The Fifteenth Amendment

Other titles in *The Constitution:*

The First Amendment
Freedom of Speech, Religion, and the Press
ISBN: 0-89490-897-9

The Second Amendment
The Right to Own Guns
ISBN:0-89490-925-8

The Fourth Amendment
Search and Seizure
ISBN: 0-89490-924-X

The Fifth Amendment
The Right to Remain Silent
ISBN: 0-89490-894-4

The Thirteenth Amendment
Ending Slavery
ISBN: 0-89490-923-1

The Fifteenth Amendment
African-American Men's Right to Vote
ISBN: 0-7660-1033-3

The Eighteenth and Twenty-First Amendments
Alcohol—Prohibition and Repeal
ISBN: 0-89490-926-6

The Nineteenth Amendment
Women's Right to Vote
ISBN: 0-89490-922-3

The Fifteenth Amendment

*African-American Men's
Right to Vote*

Susan Banfield

Enslow Publishers, Inc.

44 Fadem Road	PO Box 38
Box 699	Aldershot
Springfield, NJ 07081	Hants GU12 6BP
USA	UK

Library of Congress Cataloging-in-Publication Data

Banfield, Susan.
    The Fifteenth Amendment : African-American men's right to vote /
Susan Banfield.
        p. cm. — (The Constitution)
    Includes bibliographical references and index.
    Summary: Examines the amendment which gave African-American
men the right to vote and discusses the struggle that took place to
regain this right when it was denied.
    ISBN 0-7660-1033-3
    1. Afro-Americans—Suffrage—United States—History—Juvenile
literature. 2. United States. Constitution. 15th Amendment—History—
Juvenile literature. [1. Afro-Americans—Suffrage. 2. United States.
Constitution. 15th Amendment.] I. Title. II. Series: Constitution
(Springfield, Union County, N.J.)
KF4893.B36   1998
324.6'2'08996073—DC21   97-26318
                                               CIP
                                               AC

Printed in the United States of America

10 9 8 7 6 5 4 3 2 1

Photo Credits: AP/ Wide World Photos, p. 21; Library of Congress,
pp. 10, 13, 20, 32, 40, 43, 49, 53, 55, 57, 61, 67, 77, 87, 92.

Cover Photo: Library of Congress

Contents

Freedom Alone Is Not Enough

After the Civil War ended in 1865, African-American communities in the major cities of Virginia were exciting places to be. Former slaves, both men and women, who had been free only a few months, were flocking to Virginia's cities from all over the old South. So many came within just a few years that African Americans constituted a majority in Petersburg. In other cities, such as Richmond, Norfolk, and Lynchburg, they nearly equaled whites in numbers.[1]

Happy Reunions

Many came hoping to find husbands, wives, and children from whom they had been separated as slaves. There were many joyous reunions. Mary Jane Wilson's parents, for example, had been owned by different masters in different places. After the war, her father was able to reunite the family in Portsmouth and support them by working as a teamster in the Norfolk navy yard.[2] Others came to the cities hoping to find more opportunities than there were in rural areas. Said one of the many freed slaves who left Dinwiddie County for Richmond: "Thar a'n't no chance fo' people o' my color in the county I come from."[3]

The newly freed slaves showed a remarkable degree of cooperation and self-sufficiency. Extended families were strong, and all members of a family, even distant ones, looked out for one another's welfare. Husbands and wives, parents and children, brothers and sisters, cousins, relatives by marriage—even those who had no real relation—provided for each other. They opened bank accounts for each other and shared their living quarters. In the Mayo family of Richmond, a woman whose husband had been sold moved in, along with her son and daughter, with another "single" mother and her children. Eventually, Mrs. Mayo's son Samuel learned the plastering trade. When he was established, Samuel opened a savings account for his sister Camilla. Not long afterward, when Samuel's young wife died, Camilla cared for her brother's son and cooked for him as well as for her own husband and children.[4]

Church-Related Societies

African-American churches and church-related societies also flourished and provided help for many people. In postwar Richmond, there were over four hundred such societies.[5] They provided day schools, night classes, places for public meetings, care for the sick, assistance for those out of work, and funds for funerals and burials. Other nonchurch groups were also organized, including theater groups, social groups, and insurance societies. In Richmond, there was even an association to lend money to African Americans who wanted to build their own homes. Between eighty thousand and one hundred thousand acres of land were bought by Virginia's African Americans in the late 1860s and early 1870s.[6] Many could not have done so without the help of the Virginia Home-Building and Loan Association. A northerner who visited Richmond in 1865 commented that the African Americans in that city "seem to look for an improvement in their condition more to their own exertions and to local action, and less to the general government and the people of the North."[7]

Political Activity Begins

Along with the phenomenal growth of this local network of cooperation and mutual assistance, there was a tremendous boom in political activity in Richmond's postwar African-American community. It began almost as soon as the war was over. In large measure, it was a response to the mistreatment African Americans were continually subjected to. Shortly after the end of the war, Carl Schurz, a leader in the antislavery fight, traveled through the South in order to report on conditions there to President Andrew Johnson. Of conditions in Virginia, Schurz said: "Although the freedman is no longer considered the property of the individual master, he is considered the slave of society. . . ."[8] One African-American man complained that "Negroes coming into Yorktown from regions of Virginia and thereabout, said that they had worked all year and received no pay and were driven off the first of January."[9] Even a longtime white resident of the state commented on the injustice done to the newly freed slaves. George S. Smith, who worked with the military police, remarked that "in more than nine cases out of ten that have come up in General Patrick's office, the Negro has been right and the white man has been wrong."[10] In Richmond, a pass system was

In the days following the abolition of slavery, many African Americans seized the opportunity to form political groups. Among the goals of these groups was the improvement of the social status of the newly freed slaves.

established that required all African Americans in that city to obtain a pass from an employer in order to travel the streets freely. Any African American caught without such a pass could be thrown into jail and hired out for five dollars a month. Women looking for long-lost husbands and children looking for their parents were all suspect. None was spared the indignity of being arrested. In June 1865, eight hundred Richmond African Americans, including children, were arrested for violations of the pass system.[11]

Almost immediately, African Americans began to organize in order to protest the way they were being treated. In 1865, freed slaves held a convention in Alexandria to protest their poor treatment. In Richmond, African Americans put together a delegation to visit President Johnson personally and protest the new pass system. Their efforts paid off. The President replaced the city's mayor, and the new mayor immediately abolished the pass system. Richmond's African Americans learned that they could successfully organize to address grievances and solve problems. They soon had a host of secret political societies, often tied to the local African-American community's church and family networks. The societies provided political education, held mass meetings, called on public officials, and organized parades. Even the schools took on a political focus. The African-American pastor of one church said that in his night school, "I try to keep the school informed as to the prominent bills before Congress and at present we are reading the Constitution of the U.S. in concert. I then explain it to them as best I can and have them spell and define the important words."[12]

The Fight for the Right to Vote

As their political consciousness increased, African Americans began to call for the right to vote. Those who held the convention at Alexandria asked that they be given the vote as a remedy for their mistreatment. They said, "The only salvation for us besides the power of the Government is in the *possession of the ballot*. Give us this, and we will protect ourselves."[13] In a municipal election in Alexandria in March 1866, African Americans attempted to vote even though they were legally barred from doing so. Although their votes were not officially counted, more blacks than whites cast votes.

In the fall of 1866, the Fourteenth Amendment was passed. This guaranteed African Americans civil rights such as the right to a jury trial. By the spring of

1867, Richmond African Americans were confident that the right to vote would soon follow. The community's excitement at the prospect of at last being full participants in the political process was overwhelming. That year's Emancipation Day ceremonies were held on April 3 to mark the second anniversary of Richmond's fall to Union troops. A local African-American minister there urged hundreds of listeners to register to vote.[14] Another speaker asked the audience to "be steadfast, fight the good fight, be strong, get your diplomas. Be peaceable and wait until you get to the ballot-box before you proclaim your political sentiments."[15]

That same spring, Congress requested that each former Confederate state rewrite its constitution in order to reflect the new status of African Americans— including guaranteeing them the right to vote. On the opening day of the Republican Party Convention held to prepare delegates for the state Constitutional Convention, over three thousand African Americans waited outside Richmond's African Church hoping to be able to get in.[16] The next day, party leaders moved the convention to Capital Square in order to accommodate the crowds. In fact, so many African Americans wanted to participate in the Republican Party Convention that tobacco factories in the Richmond area were obliged to close down on opening day (August 1, 1867). They also did this whenever an important issue was to be discussed—too few employees reported to work. The Constitutional Convention itself, which ran from December 1867 to April 1868, attracted thousands of spectators daily. Most of them were African Americans.

By the time Virginia's African Americans were able at last to vote in their first federal election, participation

When they were first given the opportunity to vote in a federal election, impressive numbers of African Americans turned out at the polls to cast their ballots for the first time.

rates were extraordinarily high. The nation's new African-American citizens clearly had a love and a respect for the privilege of the ballot. Yet, those first elections in which African Americans were able to vote—and as many as 90 percent of those eligible did cast ballots—were perhaps the high point in the story of black voter participation in this country.[17] The forces working against African-American voting were very strong. Since then, both blacks and whites have had to struggle to regain the levels of voter participation of those first years after the Civil War.

In this book, you will read about how one of the strongest measures available to citizens, a constitutional amendment, was used to guarantee African Americans their voting rights. In spite of this amendment, however, African Americans were all but stripped of the privilege of the ballot box. After almost a century of struggle, African-American voter participation is still not on a par with what it was back in the 1860s. It is a sad story in many ways, but it is also a story of courage and determination. Hopefully, it is a story to inspire those on whose shoulders the ongoing struggle will rest in the years to come.

The Vote—A Hard-Earned Right

Today most people in the United States take the right to vote for granted. Politicians have to work hard to get people of all races to go to the polls. This attitude toward voting is a recent and far-from-universal phenomenon. For centuries, the majority of men and women the world over had no say in how they were governed. They had no voting privileges whatsoever.

Voting in Ancient Cultures

In ancient times, most people were ruled by kings or similar rulers who had the power to make decisions as to how those under them should be governed. There were, however, a few cases in which people in ancient societies had significant voting rights. The ancient Greeks are widely regarded as the first civilization in which people were able to participate in government through voting. In both Sparta and Athens, all male citizens over a certain age were able to take part in the assembly. This group passed laws and made decisions for the people of the city-state. In one sense, the level of political participation among the ancient Greeks was even higher than it is in present-day America. Citizens cast their own votes on the various proposed laws and other matters that came before the assembly. They did not simply elect representatives who would vote for them as we do in this country. However, not all men who lived in a city-state could be counted as citizens and thus eligible to participate in this way. A man's ability to participate was tied to his ownership of land, and no women could take part. Even Plato, the well-known Greek philosopher who wrote extensively on the nature of the ideal state, did not believe that all men were qualified to take part in government. He believed that the privilege of voting should be limited. Aristotle, another well-known Greek philosopher, was hesitant about letting artisans and tradesmen become citizens and voters.

The ancient Romans also had a senate and an assembly that made decisions for the Republic. All citizens of the Republic had the right to vote. Citizens included artisans, shopkeepers, laborers, and wealthy landowners. But around the time of Jesus Christ, the Roman Republic was replaced by the Roman Empire. The absolute rule of the emperors replaced democracy. Under the emperors, only members of the oldest and wealthiest families were still able to vote and participate in government. This they did through the senate, the legislative body that was limited to members of Rome's noble class.

During the Middle Ages, voting and representative government were rare. Kings had groups of men who advised them. In many cases, however, the position of adviser to a king was an appointed office, not an elected one. England was the first country to develop a tradition of voting and popular participation in

government. When King Edward I summoned
Parliament in 1295, he did so with the words "let that
which toucheth all be approved by all."[1] Edward's
Parliament included representatives from the new
towns and cities, as well as nobility and clergy. These
representatives were elected. Still, voting was far from
a universal right. In 1430, a law limited the right to
vote for members of Parliament to men who owned
land worth forty shillings a year in rental value. A
major reason given for the law was that "manslaugh-
ters, riots, batteries [beatings] and divisions" were sure
to take place if "people of small substance, or of not
value" were allowed to vote.[2] There were other restrictions on voting as well. Voters had to be male, over the
age of twenty-one, and had to have been assessed for
taxes twelve months before an election. Voting was
regarded not as a right but as a privilege.

The restriction of voting, especially to men who
owned property, remained in practice for centuries.
Various reasons for the property requirement were
given over the years. Some political theorists believed
that property holders had virtues that would be of
special benefit to the state—independence, stability,
good character, respect for personal and property rights
of others. William Blackstone, the famous English
legal theorist who wrote in the 1700s, maintained that
voting was in fact a right. Still, he upheld property
qualifications. He gave the following reason: the "true
reason of requiring any qualification with regard to
property in voters is to exclude such persons as are in
so mean a situation as to be esteemed to have no will
of their own."[3] In other words, Blackstone feared that
rural tenant farmers or poor urban workers could easily be led to vote as their landlord or employer wanted
them to.

Early U.S. Settlers

In colonial America in the late 1700s, early settlers, for the most part, continued the practice of restricting voting to men who owned property. Usually, it had to be of a certain minimum acreage or value. The House of Burgesses in colonial Virginia declared that:

> Whereas the laws of England grant a voice in such election only to such as by their estates real or personal have interest enough to tie them to the endeavor of the public good, it is hereby enacted that none but freeholders and housekeepers . . . shall hereafter have a voice in the election of any Burgesses in this country.[4]

However, between 50 and 90 percent of adult males in the colonies met the property qualifications for voting—depending on location.[5] This was because land was plentiful and inexpensive in America.

A greater number of men in the colonies had become used to being able to vote. In addition, new ideas circulating in the period before the Revolutionary War led some people to think that even the restrictions that still existed should be done away with. It was hard to maintain that all men are created equal, and then grant the vote to some but not to others. Several colonies did away with their property qualifications. Still, there was much debate over the wisdom of universal manhood suffrage, or, granting the right to vote to all males over a certain age. At the time the Constitution was approved in 1788, it said nothing about qualifications for voting. Instead, this difficult question was left to the states to decide.

As the United States grew in the first half of the nineteenth century, the nation gradually moved toward universal manhood suffrage, voting rights for all men. States rewrote their constitutions. They replaced the property-holding qualification with a qualification that voters also be taxpayers. Sometimes they even did away with such qualifications altogether. The development of the western part of the United States helped push the rest of the nation in this direction. In part, this was because elections in territories needed to be held before titles to land could be determined. Also, men and women on the frontier tended to be more democratic. Of the states admitted to the Union between 1796 and 1821, three had a tax-paying requirement for voting; the rest had voting privileges for all white men.[6] Some prominent statesmen, however, continued to support property qualifications. For example, an aging John Adams declared: "Our ancestors have made a pecuniary [monetary] qualification necessary . . . for electors, and all the wise men of the world have agreed in the same thing."[7] By 1840, however, Rhode Island was the only American state that limited voting to property holders.[8]

Voting Rights for White Men

By the 1850s, Americans stood squarely behind the idea of voting rights for all white men. They boasted of their democratic electoral system, which was much more inclusive than those found in Europe at that time. Europeans had toyed with the idea of voting rights for all men around the time of the French Revolution, in the late eighteenth century. But the French Revolution had a far less optimistic outcome than did its American counterpart. This caused many in Europe to rethink the idea of granting the right to vote to all men. "We say, and we justly say, that it is not by mere numbers, but by property and intelligence that the nation should be governed," declared the English statesman Thomas Macaulay in 1831.[9] Most

European nations did not achieve universal manhood suffrage until the last quarter of the nineteenth century.

Most people regarded the establishment of universal manhood suffrage as an accomplishment to be proud of. It must be remembered, however, that at least half of the adult population—namely, all women—were still disqualified from voting under such rules. The fight for voting rights for women was a long and hard one. Women began to ask for the right to vote in the years before the Civil War (1861–1865). Both in the United States and in England they held marches and demonstrations and wrote pamphlets and books. Women worked tirelessly for decades trying to

Winning the right to vote was quite difficult for women as well. It was not until 1920—with the passage of the Nineteenth Amendment—that suffrage became truly "universal" in the United States.

get governments to grant them the vote. It was not until 1918, in England, and 1920, in the United States, that women won this hard-fought battle. In other countries, the struggle continued even longer. Neither France nor Italy granted women the right to vote until after World War II, in the late 1940s.

For the most part, this steady march toward voting rights for all took place in the developed nations of the West. In other parts of the world, people—both men and women—have had to fight throughout the twentieth century, and are still fighting, for the right to vote.

On April 26, 1994, lines of people, sometimes seeming to stretch for miles, dotted the countryside all over South Africa. These streams of people consisted

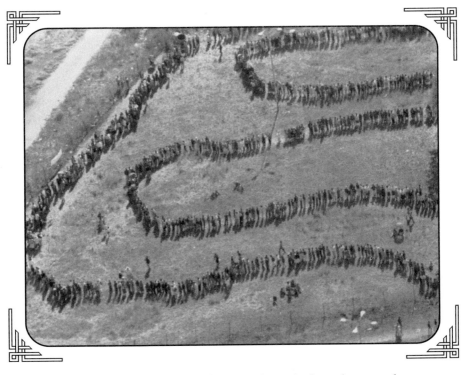

After enduring years of being denied their basic rights under apartheid, black South Africans line up by the thousands to exercise their right to vote for the first time.

of both men and women, young and old. What was the occasion? This was the day of the first election in South Africa's history in which blacks were allowed to vote. All who possibly could made their way to the polls. Those who were too old or sick to walk were carried or pulled in carts. Many waited on line for four, five, or even eight hours to cast their ballots. In some cases, people slept overnight to hold their place in line for the next day. "I feel happy and energetic," commented one seventy-five-year-old woman who voted for the first time in her life. "I think I could throw this cane away. The way I feel I have no words to say."[10] Thousands of other South African blacks echoed her sense of elation. To these people, the day of their first ballot was one of the high points of their lives.

African Americans in the United States are no strangers to the struggles of twentieth-century black South Africans or of turn-of-the-century American and English women. Thousands of African Americans in the not-so-distant past have experienced the jubilation of being able to vote for the first time. In the following chapters, you will read about the tremendous obstacles African Americans have had to overcome in order to secure their right to the ballot.

3

The Struggle for Freedom

In August 1619, the first Africans arrived in what would one day be the United States. A ship pulled into the harbor at Jamestown, Virginia, and its captain offered to exchange for food some Africans he had captured from a Spanish ship.[1] These first African Americans were not slaves, however. Nor were they regarded by the white settlers as belonging to an inferior race. The first Africans to come to North America came, for the most part, on the same footing as poor whites. They came as indentured servants. Indentured servants owed their services to a master for a given number of years. After that time, they were given their freedom.

A Short Period of Equality

For the first forty years or so of Virginia's colonial history, black settlers lived side by side with whites on a basis of equality. Blacks owned land, voted, held public office, and even had servants of their own. It was much the same in the other colonies. In New York, the first Africans arrived in 1626, servants of the Dutch West Indian Company. They were all granted their freedom in 1644.[2]

Growth of Southern Plantations

This period of equality was short-lived, however. By the 1660s, the plantations in the southern colonies had grown tremendously. There was a rapidly expanding international market for rice and tobacco. The plantation owners' need for laborers became acute, and the use of indentured servants had limitations. These men and women had to be given their freedom after a set period of time. Others had to be found to take their place. Also, when servants were freed, their masters were obliged to give them clothes and a small sum of money or a piece of land.[3] Instead, the plantation owners wanted slaves for life. Brief attempts were made to enslave Native Americans. But it was too easy for them to escape because they knew the countryside.[4] The colonists then turned to Africans as a possible solution to their labor shortage. There were earlier examples to support this practice. Spanish and Portuguese settlers in South America had been using African slave labor for over two hundred years.

At first, slavery was still not a permanent, absolute state. An English law said that "a slave who had been christened or baptized became 'infranchised.'"[5] There is evidence that the law was abided by in the colonies. One black man, John Phillip, was allowed to testify in the trial of a white man in the early years of the Virginia colony only because he had been baptized.[6]

By 1682, however, Virginia had passed a law that made Africans slaves for life and that struck down the old English law that granted freedom to those who converted to Christianity, "making slaves of all persons of non-Christian nationalities thereafter coming into the colony, whether they came by sea or by land and whether or not they had been converted to Christianity after capture."[7] Other colonies soon followed Virginia's lead, and the seeds of centuries of prejudice and racism were thus sown. The trade in men, women, and children from the west coast of Africa was stepped up markedly. By 1710, there were some fifty thousand Africans in the colonies. By the time of the American Revolution, there would be some five hundred thousand. [8]

Early Slave Trade

In the first decades of the slave trade, back in the 1400s and 1500s, Africans and Europeans had regarded one another largely as equals. The European explorers of Africa were impressed with that continent's cities and regal princes. Members of Africa's ruling class traveled to Europe to study. Africans and Europeans viewed one another as trading partners. But, by the 1700s, the relationship had become much more one-sided and exploitative. Africans had for centuries enslaved each other. Prisoners captured in wars had often been taken as slaves. But slaves had traditionally been treated like members of their master's family. With encouragement from Europeans, African rulers began to sell their slaves. Some even conducted kidnapping raids in order to gather more slaves to trade.[9]

The men and women who were sold into slavery were treated as abominably as it is possible to conceive. They were marched overland sometimes hundreds of miles to the coast. There they were inspected like livestock, branded, and packed into ships like sardines.

"Their lodging rooms below the deck," wrote a minister who observed them firsthand,

> are sometimes more than five feet high and sometimes less; and this height is divided toward the middle for the slaves lie in two rows, one above the other, . . . close to each other like books upon a shelf. I have known them so close that the shelf would not easily contain one more.[10]

Although English law set a limit on the number of slaves each ship could hold, such numbers meant little. One slave ship called the *Brookes* was allowed to carry 454 slaves. It was reported by its surgeon to have carried six hundred and more.[11] During the course of the six- to ten-week voyage, many died of disease. Quite a few tried to commit suicide; others went crazy.

A Grim Existence

Those who managed to survive the passage faced a grim existence. Most worked long and hard hours in the fields. They were increasingly scorned and ostracized by the white men and women they worked for. In Virginia, by the late 1600s, a white person who mingled socially with blacks faced censure by fellow colonists.[12] Overseers regarded the black men and women in their charge much like animals. One remarked that breaking in a "new Negro" required "more hard Discipline than a young Spaniel."[13]

The American Revolution did have some positive effect on the colonists' attitudes toward Africans. In part as a result of the widespread talk of independence, freedom, and human rights, a number of colonies passed antislave-trade measures in the years before the war. Some individuals took steps to free their slaves. One such person was Richard Randolph. He wrote to the man managing his estate, "I have only to say that I want not a single Negro for any other purpose than his immediate liberation. I consider every individual thus unshackled as the source of future generations, not to say nations, of freedmen."[14] In the first years of the new nation, slavery was largely abolished in the North. One after the other, these new states passed laws granting slaves their freedom, either immediately or after a set number of years. One delegate to the Massachusetts convention, held to ratify the new nation's constitution, remarked that the slave trade "has received a mortal wound, and will die of consumption."[15] Abolition societies were founded in the Middle Atlantic and New England states. These groups worked to end the slave trade and slavery in places where it was still allowed. They also provided education for African Americans who had been recently freed.

Still, the attitude of most white Americans toward their black neighbors was one of prejudice and often hostility. Even Thomas Jefferson, author of the Declaration of Independence, was wary of the prospect of an America in which all African Americans were free. "Nothing is more certainly written in the book of fate, than that these people are to be free; nor is it less certain that the two races, equally free, cannot live in the same government," said Jefferson.[16] As the years wore on, the northern states, where most free African Americans resided, one by one took away their right to vote. By the eve of the Civil War, African Americans were denied the vote in all but five of the New England states. (Since only 6 percent of northern African Americans lived in these five states, this statistic is even less impressive.)[17]

In the South, it was worse. Several years after the end of the Revolutionary War, Eli Whitney invented his famous cotton gin. The cotton gin, along with other advances in the manufacture of textiles, led to huge growth in the cultivation of cotton in the southern states. The demand for slaves to harvest and process the cotton also grew as a result. By the late 1850s, there were nearly 4 million African-American slaves in the United States.[18]

The African Americans who worked the large cotton plantations led, for the most part, lives of extreme degradation. They worked from before dawn until well into the night, under the threat of a ready whip. Their manner toward their masters had to reflect their total subjugation at all times. Wrote former slave Charles Ball: "[We] were always obliged to approach the door of the mansion, in the most humble and supplicating manner, with our hats in our hands, and the most subdued and beseeching language in our mouths. . . ."[19] Any deviation from the prescribed routine was likely to result in physical punishment. Flogging was one of the most common punishments. A slave could receive as many as fifty to seventy-five lashes for an offense. One Mississippi planter once gave a slave one thousand lashes. On many other occasions, slaves were branded, stabbed, tarred and feathered, or burned.[20]

In addition to physical punishment, elaborate sets of regulations, known as "slave codes," were enacted to keep slaves ignorant and under the thumb of their white masters. Slaves were forbidden to assemble in groups larger than five. They could not leave their plantation without a pass. They could not hold a religious meeting without a white witness present, nor could they blow horns or beat drums. They could not even be taught to read.

As slavery became a central feature of southern life, white southerners developed a variety of rationales defending it and the notion of white superiority/black inferiority that underlay it. Many argued that slavery was supported by the Bible. John C. Calhoun was a prominent southern senator of the early 1800s. He maintained that slavery was a great institution that benefited all involved—especially the slaves.

> Experience had shown that the existing relation between [black and white] secured the peace and happiness of both. Each had improved; the inferior greatly; so much so, that it had attained a degree of civilization never before attained by the black race in any age or country. Under no other relation could they coexist together.[21]

One of the most widely read propagandists for slavery was George Fitzhugh of Virginia. He argued that African Americans were better off as slaves than they would be if left to themselves in a capitalist society.

> We do not set children and women free because they are not capable of taking care of themselves, not equal to the constant struggle of society. To set them free would be to give the lamb to the wolf to take care of. Society would quickly devour them. . . . But half of mankind are but grown-up children, and liberty is as fatal to them as it would be to children. . . . Slaves never die of hunger, scarcely ever feel want.[22]

Life in the North

African Americans in the northern states fared better but still had to contend with massive injustice. Alexis de Tocqueville was a French statesman who traveled extensively in the United States in the 1830s. He noted that "[t]he prejudice of race appears to be stronger in the states that have abolished slavery than in those where it still exists. . . ."[23] Even Abraham Lincoln, the United States president most commonly associated with the advancement of African Americans, declared that "[t]here is a physical difference between the white and black races which I believe will forever forbid the two races living together on terms of social and political equality."[24]

It was this pervasive prejudice that enabled the country to enact federal laws and to make weighty legal judgments that were most unjust in their effect on African Americans. In 1850, Congress passed the Fugitive Slave Law. This compelled state and local officials to cooperate with the federal government in capturing runaway slaves and returning them to their owners. In 1857, the United States Supreme Court handed down a decision in the *Dred Scott* case. The Court declared slaves and their descendants to be property rather than citizens. This effectively denied ordinary civil rights to all slaves.

"Let Southern oppressors tremble—let their secret abettors tremble—let their Northern apologists tremble—let all the enemies of the persecuted black tremble."[25] These were the challenging words of William Lloyd Garrison, a leader of a newly energized abolitionist movement that emerged in the middle of the nineteenth century. Since the time of the Revolutionary War, there had been abolitionist societies. But as slavery became more and more deeply entrenched in the South, there was a sharp increase in the number and the power of the voices that could be heard decrying its evils. Both white and black abolitionists urged their fellow citizens to do away with slavery immediately. They also urged the end of discrimination toward free African Americans.

Seeds of the Civil War

By 1860, the conflict between the antislavery and proslavery camps had grown so fierce it helped to lead the country into a brutal and bloody war. The Civil War, however, resulted in the first great triumph for African Americans—Lincoln's Emancipation Proclamation. On January 1, 1863, Lincoln proclaimed that all slaves in states or parts of states still fighting against the United States would henceforth be free. Although this did not include all slaves, African Americans all over the nation, both slave and free, celebrated.

At the outbreak of the Civil War, there were close to 4.5 million African Americans in the United States. Nearly 4 million of these were slaves, and the vast majority of them, both slave and free, lived in the South.[26] In three southern states—South Carolina, Mississippi, and Louisiana—African Americans formed a majority of the population. In two other states—Virginia and North Carolina—African Americans accounted for 40 percent of the population.[27] The changes that were initiated by the Emancipation Proclamation would be mammoth indeed.

The Reconstruction Era

By the end of the war, in 1864, the changes were already well under way. Reconstruction (1865–1877) is the name commonly given to the period of growth following the Civil War. During the early years, African Americans formed a wide variety of new social organizations. Now they were free to meet in large groups without white supervision. They organized trade associations, temperance clubs (clubs devoted to stopping the use of alcohol), drama societies, debating

Even though the slaves had been freed following the end of the Civil War, abolitionists such as Frederick Douglass felt that many obstacles remained before African Americans would be accepted as equal members of society.

societies, burial societies, and, most importantly, political organizations.

It seemed the newly freed slaves were hungry for two things. One was education. Booker T. Washington said of the Reconstruction period:

> It was a whole race trying to go to school. Few were too young, and none too old, to make the attempt to learn. As fast as any kind of teachers could be secured, not only were day schools filled, but night schools as well.[28]

As much as they wanted to learn to read and write, African Americans also wanted to be politically active. Political clubs and organizations sprang up all over. Debates, rallies, parades, and meetings were held on a regular basis. A typical meeting in Charleston, South Carolina, was described by a white observer. At night, the city's blacks gathered "with lighted torches, lanterns, and transparencies and went, with bands of music, and with songs of liberty, to the houses of the prominent political men . . . drinking in at every point words of encouragement and hope."[29] Women as well as men were active participants.

The Union League

One of the biggest, most influential political organizations to flourish among newly freed slaves was the Union League. The Union League was originally founded by whites in Philadelphia during the Civil War. League meetings provided political education along abolitionist and Republican lines. After the war ended, the Union League spread through the South. One of its main aims was to win the allegiance of African Americans. Supreme Court Chief Justice Salmon Chase traveled through the South to report on the situation there to President Johnson. He noted that "everywhere throughout the country colored citizens are organizing Union Leagues."[30]

Leaders quickly emerged to guide and inspire the new African-American political community. Members included teachers, preachers, and others—mostly ex-slaves. These early leaders were looked up to more for personal qualities such as good sense and high principles than for education, political experience, or social status. Union League organizer Thomas Allen was a typical African-American leader of the time. Allen, an ex-slave, was a Baptist preacher, a shoemaker, and a farmer (though he owned no land of his own). He knew how to read. He was trusted enough by the African Americans in his community that eventually he was elected as a Georgia state lawmaker. "In my country the colored people came to me for instructions," Allen said of how he got started, "and I gave them the best instructions I could. I took the *New York Tribune* and other papers, and in that way I found out a great deal, and I told them whatever I thought was right."[31] Many of the new African-American leaders were largely self-educated. John Lynch worked in a photographer's studio in Mississippi just across an alleyway from a white school. He used to take time off and look out through the studio window and into the white schoolroom across the way. He was actually able to keep up with the class and mastered a number of subjects.[32]

Southern whites were extremely suspicious of any activity on the part of the newly freed slaves. They were especially distrustful of political activity. Whites in South Carolina felt quite threatened by the prospect of politically active African Americans. In fact, they held a convention in 1867 to stage a formal protest. They said, in part:

We . . . enter our most solemn protest against the policy
of investing the negro with political rights. The black
man is what God and nature and circumstances have
made him. . . . The fact is patent [obvious] to all that the
negro is utterly unfitted to exercise the highest
functions of the citizen.[33]

Whites in the South treated blacks savagely and
thought little of it. They paid them outrageously low
wages, killed the few cattle or hogs they were able to
buy, and often beat or killed blacks themselves, for no
reason. "Men who are honorable in their dealings with
their white neighbors, will cheat a Negro without feel-
ing a single twinge of their honor," reported Carl
Schurz of his travels down South. "To kill a Negro
they do not deem murder . . . to take the property away
from a Negro, they do not consider robbery."[34]

It was not long before southern whites' desire to
repress the newly freed blacks was formalized. Within
months of the end of the Civil War, most southern
states had passed what became known as "black
codes." These laws bore a striking resemblance to the
old slave codes. Most forbid blacks to assemble in
groups, to be on the streets at night after a certain
hour, to preach or speak publicly without special per-
mission, or to follow any but a limited number of
trades. They clearly made of the newly freed slaves an
inferior class of citizens.

The Thirteenth Amendment

The Thirteenth Amendment to the Constitution was
passed in 1865. It was meant to put an end to slavery.
It said that "Congress shall have power to enforce this
article by appropriate legislation." Southerners, however, did not want anyone to force them to respect the
political rights of African Americans. During the early
years of Reconstruction, the federal government did

not put many restrictions on southerners. Under the leadership of President Andrew Johnson, just about all the former Confederate states had to do to be readmitted to the Union was ratify the Thirteenth Amendment (freeing the slaves), repeal their acts of secession, and let go of their claims to war debts. President Johnson apparently did not have a very high view of African Americans. "The negroes are not the equals of white Americans . . . and are not entitled by any right, natural or acquired to participate in the government of this country," the president remarked at one point.[35] While President Johnson headed up Reconstruction, the southern states sent seventy-four former Confederates to Congress, including former generals and cabinet members.[36] Living conditions for African Americans in some places were hardly any better than they had been before the war.

Up to this point in American history, people's civil rights had been regarded as the exclusive concern of the states. It was up to the state governments to define and protect these rights. President Johnson used such a position to justify not requiring the newly admitted southern states to grant the vote to African Americans. In his 1865 annual message to Congress, he said that this was a question to be decided by the states. This was what the Constitution prescribed. This all changed dramatically, however, as Reconstruction progressed.

The first step on the road to federal control of citizens' civil rights came with the passage of the Civil Rights Bill of 1866. This bill gave the federal government the responsibility for extending the protection of the Bill of Rights to *all* Americans. The first ten amendments to the Constitution are known as the Bill of Rights. They were meant to secure personal freedoms not specifically outlined in the Constitution. Neither the Bill of Rights nor the Civil Rights Bill included the right to vote. Voting was still regarded more as a privilege than as a right.

Violence Erupts

Progress in government protection of African Americans' rights was slowed by two bloody race riots that took place in May 1866. One was in Memphis, Tennessee, and the other was in New Orleans, Louisiana. While the origins of the two riots are hazy, in both cases the police were reported to be actively hunting down African Americans. The Memphis chief of police is reported to have told his men, "Boys, I want you to go ahead and kill the last damned one of the . . . race, and burn up the cradle."[37] Witnesses of the New Orleans riot said that "at least nine-tenths of the casualties were perpetrated by the police and citizens by stabbing and smashing in the heads of many who had already been wounded or killed by policemen."[38] In Memphis, forty-six African Americans were killed and more than eighty were wounded. In New Orleans, there were thirty-four African Americans killed, and over two hundred wounded.[39] Both riots were massive and cruel attacks on African Americans. Many people, however, took them as a sign that African Americans were not civilized enough to be entrusted with the right to vote.

The Fourteenth Amendment

In 1868, the Fourteenth Amendment to the Constitution was passed. This amendment is revered to this day for its famous "equal protection clause." It deals with search and arrest warrants. It also strengthens the Civil Rights Act by giving a constitutional guarantee to a number of rights. These rights are promised to all citizens regardless of race. However, voting rights are not part of the amendment.

In March 1867, control of Reconstruction passed from the president to the Congress. The president had been inclined to turn much of that control back to the states. With the passage of Congress's First Reconstruction Act, responsibility for the rights, indeed the very lives, of southern Americans was placed squarely in the hands of the federal government.

The act prescribed extreme measures to ensure that the rights of African Americans were protected. First, it divided the South into five military districts. Each was under the command of an Army officer. To make sure that blacks (and poor whites) had food, shelter, and a chance to go to school, the act created the Freedmen's Bureau. The bureau issued millions of rations, staffed hospitals, and ran schools. In the area of education alone, the bureau spent over $5 million between June 1865 and September 1871. By 1870, there were 3,300 teachers and 149,581 students in bureau schools.[40] W.E.B. Du Bois was an important leader of African-American protest in the United States. He called the Freedmen's Bureau "the most extraordinary and far-reaching institution of social uplift that America has ever attempted."[41]

In perhaps its most extreme prescription, the First Reconstruction Act also insisted that African Americans be given the right to vote. It set new criteria for readmission into the Union. The new rules were much more stringent than those of President Johnson. Among them was that a state guarantee voting rights to all male citizens aged twenty-one and older, "of whatever race, color, or previous condition."[42] Each southern state was to hold a constitutional convention to draft a new constitution. The constitution then had to be approved by Congress before the state could be readmitted. Delegates to these state conventions also had to be elected by voters "of whatever race, color, or previous condition. . . ."[43]

African Americans Involved in Politics

Thus began one of the great experiments in America's history. Following the passage of the Reconstruction Act, a massive campaign was begun to register African-American voters and educate them in the ways of politics. Thousands of meetings were held throughout the South. Political materials were read aloud at picnics, balls, and gatherings of every sort. Lecturers traveled from town to town bringing the message of the Republican Party to the freed slaves. Registrars instructed them in American history. Political rallies became so popular that planters complained that their African-American field hands were neglecting their work to attend. One historian has said of the campaign that "no more impressive political operation has ever been conducted in the history of the country."[44] By autumn of 1867, more than seven hundred thousand African Americans in the southern states had registered to vote. In five states, more blacks were registered than whites.[45] One thousand African Americans who had decided to leave the United States for Liberia in 1866 and early 1867 changed their minds. They decided to remain in the United States once the Reconstruction Act was passed. They were too excited by the prospect of voting.[46] African-American turnout for the fall of 1867 and other early elections approached 90 percent in some places.[47] Tens of thousands of freed slaves went to the polls, often

African Americans found initial success in politics once given the right to vote. Many held significant memberships in legislatures such as South Carolina's, and earned praise from outside observers.

celebrating the occasion with banners, bands, picnics, and other festivities.

During the winter and spring of 1867 to 1868, southern African Americans, many still illiterate and most just a few short years away from slavery, voted for the first time. They also came together with their white neighbors to elect delegates and draft new state constitutions. It must be noted that many white southerners stayed away from the polls out of protest. It is still remarkable, however, that southern voters elected a total of 265 African-American delegates to the state conventions. Nearly half of them had been born slaves.[48] In South Carolina, African Americans accounted for 61 percent of the delegates.[49]

How did these first African-American elected officials fare? Southern whites were sure they would fail miserably. A week before South Carolina's constitutional convention, a group of white citizens declared, "The fact is patent to all . . . that the Negro is utterly unfitted to exercise the highest function of a citizen."[50] In fact, just the opposite proved to be the case. As the South Carolina convention got under way, the *Charleston Daily News* reported:

> Beyond question, the best men in the convention are the colored members. Considering . . . their imperfect acquaintance with parliamentary law, they have displayed, for the most part, remarkable moderation and dignity. . . . They have assembled neither to pull wires like some, nor to make money like others; but to legislate for the welfare of the race to which they belong.[51]

In fact, the document that they came up with contained many modern ideas. It established an integrated school system and abolished corporal punishment and imprisonment for minor crimes such as debt. It also made the government responsible for the sick, the elderly, and the poor. The new constitution was considered so sound that, even after conservative whites took over the state government, they kept it for eighteen years. Even when they did change the Constitution, in 1895, they kept many of its features. Similar stories can be told of the other southern states as well. A political organizer who worked in North Carolina remarked that, "there is but little if any difference in the talents of the two races."[52]

As African Americans took to the polls, political leaders began to emerge from among their ranks. The first African-American politicians in the South were men of great character and courage. They quite literally took their lives into their hands when they announced their candidacy. At least 10 percent of the African Americans who served in the constitutional conventions of 1867 to 1868 were victims of violence; seven of them were murdered.[53] In one Alabama county, four of the five delegates to the state convention were killed. The fifth barely escaped with his life after more than 265 gunshots were fired into his house.[54]

Newly Elected Officials

The backgrounds of the newly elected African-American politicians were extremely varied. Some, like Francis L. Cardoza and Robert Elliott, were highly educated. Cardoza was a free-born black of Jewish, Indian, and African ancestry. He was educated in Scotland and England, and attended England's prestigious Eton College. Others had much more humble backgrounds. Robert DeLarge was a Charleston tailor with limited education. He served as state lawmaker. Samuel J. Lee, South Carolina's

THE FIRST COLORED SENATOR AND REPRESENTATIVES.

In the 41st and 42nd Congress of the United States.

During the Reconstruction period, several African Americans were elected as the representatives or senators of their home states.

speaker of the house, had worked on farms and in lumber mills and was self-educated. By the end of Reconstruction, two of these African-American political leaders, Blanche Bruce and Hiram Revels, both of Mississippi, had been sent to serve in the United States Senate. Twenty had been elected to seats in the House of Representatives. Senator James G. Blaine said of his African-American fellow legislators, "The colored men who took seats in both Senate and House did not appear ignorant or helpless. They were as a rule studious, earnest, ambitious men, whose public conduct . . . would be honorable to any race."[55]

It seemed to some as though the great experiment with African-American voting rights was a huge success. There was a sense that African-American participation in the nation's political life was here to stay. Many more, however, were all too aware how fragile a victory this might prove to be.

The Amendment Is Passed

W hat looked like an overnight national transformation in 1867 turned out to be anything but that. The decision to allow African Americans to vote was not the sudden act it seemed. Rather, it was the outcome of a movement that was several years old. It was a movement that had gradually but steadily been gaining strength. Nor was the decision as final and secure as it seemed at first. People all over the country, both black and white, northern and southern, were keenly aware that the delicate balance of forces that first made mass African-American voting rights possible could be upset at any moment. Legal safeguards of the decision needed to be enacted.

The movement to allow African Americans to vote had to begin almost from ground zero. At the end of the Civil War, there was little support for the idea. In 1864, only five northern states allowed African Americans to vote.[1] In 1865, *The New York Times* came out as completely opposed to the idea.[2] Between 1865 and 1867, referendums on the question of African-American voting rights were held in a number of northern states. Most of these were defeated. In 1868, there were still just eight (out of sixteen) northern states that allowed African Americans to vote.[3]

A typical northern attitude on the question at that time was that of Senator James Grimes of Iowa, who said:

> As to the Negro I have not changed my opinion from the beginning. I think I shall come pretty nearly to the measure of my duty when I secure him his rights as a party in the courts, as a witness on the stand, as a scholar in the school, and as a christian in the church . . . but I am under the impression that he can live some years and so can we without bestowing on him the elective franchise.[4]

Some thought the newly freed slaves should vote someday but not yet. Even Thaddeus Stevens, leader of the Radical Republicans, was of this mind. The Radical Republicans were the party that had pushed for congressional Reconstruction. Still, Stevens remarked, "I do not therefore want to grant them this privilege [the vote] for some years . . . four or five years hence, when the freedmen shall have been made free indeed, when they shall have become intelligent enough . . . ."[5] Even Abraham Lincoln, traditionally regarded as a great friend of the slave, was not sure African Americans other than those who were demonstrably intelligent or who had faithfully served in the Union Army, should receive the privilege of the ballot. In 1864, Lincoln "cautiously suggested" to the state of Louisiana that it consider "whether some of the colored people may not be let in, as for instance, the very intelligent, and especially those who have fought gallantly in our ranks."[6]

Southern whites were shocked at the prospect of

African-American voters. One southern man said his contemporaries regarded African-American voting rights as "one of the things they imagine they will never submit to . . . too monstrous a proposition even to debate. . . ."[7] Even some southern African Americans at first wondered whether their people were ready for the ballot box. Said one educated southern African American, "I don't want the colored people to vote for five years. Here, and for twenty miles away they'll vote right, but farther off they will vote for 'Mass William' and 'Mass John' to get their good will."[8]

However, from the outset, many African Americans hungered for the right to vote. It was largely with them that the movement for African-American suffrage got its start. In 1863, the famous African-American abolitionist Frederick Douglass addressed a meeting of the Anti-Slavery Society. He discussed the importance of voting rights for African Americans. He said:

> I understand the anti-slavery societies of this country to be based on two principles, . . . first, the freedom of the blacks of this country; and second, the elevation of them. . . . It is said that we are ignorant; I admit it. But if we know enough to be hung, we know enough to vote. If the negro knows enough to pay taxes to support the Government, he knows enough to vote. If he knows enough to shoulder a musket and fight for the flag, fight for the Government, he knows enough to vote.[9]

(All told, thirty-seven thousand African Americans died in defense of the Union. Seventeen African-American soldiers and sailors received the Congressional Medal of Honor for outstanding bravery in the Civil War.[10]) Douglass pleaded with the Anti-Slavery Society not to disband when the war was over. Its work was not done, he said. "Without this [the vote] his liberty is a mockery . . . for in fact if he is not the slave of an individual master, he is the slave of society."[11] In 1864, delegates from eighteen states gathered in Syracuse, New York, to work to obtain voting rights for African Americans.[12] In the spring and summer of 1865, African Americans held numerous mass meetings and marched in parades, focusing on their demand for voting and other civil rights. In 1866, African Americans in Alexandria, Virginia, were so eager to vote that they tried to vote in a local election.

Gradually, more and more whites came to support the cause of blacks' right to vote. By the middle of 1864, a few abolitionists, such as Wendell Phillips, were insisting that Reconstruction would not be complete unless African Americans were given education, access to land, and the vote. In the fall of 1865, well-known abolitionist, Senator Charles Sumner, declared, "Slavery has been abolished in name, that is all. It is essential that all men be hailed as equal before the law; and this enfranchisement must be both political and civil."[13]

Whites Support Blacks' Right to Vote

By 1866, the issue of voting rights for African Americans had a prominent place on lawmakers' agendas. During campaigns for that year's elections, it was hotly debated. In December 1866, Congress passed a bill giving African Americans in the District of Columbia the right to vote. That year, too, the idea of a special amendment guaranteeing African Americans their voting rights was suggested for the first time. The Fourteenth Amendment contained only indirect support for African-American voting rights. States would be penalized by having the number of their

Senator Charles Sumner, a well-known abolitionist, felt that without the right to vote, African Americans were still slaves to a system over which they had no control.

representatives in Congress reduced in proportion to the number of people to whom they denied the vote.

The big leap forward came the next year, in 1867, with the passage of the First Reconstruction Act. As you have read, the act required the southern states to grant African Americans the vote as a condition for being readmitted to the Union. It also mandated that southern African Americans be allowed to vote for delegates to their state's constitutional convention. But that same year, the fall election results seemed to indicate that support for the idea of universal African-American voting rights was spotty at best. The Republicans were the party that championed the cause of African-American voting rights. They lost many seats in Congress and two gubernatorial races in 1867. As a result of this poor showing, in 1868, the party decided to nominate General Ulysses S. Grant for president rather than Chief Justice Salmon Chase, who was a champion of African-American voting rights.[14]

In spite of this setback, the momentum that had started to build for the idea of African-American votes continued to gather strength. In the opening days of the thirty-ninth Congress, in 1867, six proposals designed to guarantee African Americans the right to vote were put forth.[15] In 1868, Republicans started to realize that most African Americans would be likely to vote for candidates of their party. Some measure ensuring that all African Americans were allowed to vote would be to their political advantage. With this realization, the campaign to secure African-American voting rights stepped up noticeably. In November 1868, the Republicans again made a somewhat weak showing in the national elections. Just days later, the *Philadelphia Press* made the first explicit public call for a Fifteenth Amendment guaranteeing African Americans the right to vote.

> Let the Fortieth Congress . . . propose an amendment to the Constitution conferring the power to vote for national purposes and offices on colored men, under equal conditions with white men. . . . [Thus] where the colored men vote, there the cause of Republicanism is entirely safe, and will be.[16]

The idea of the amendment caught on quickly. Many who jumped on the bandwagon were Republicans. They saw African-American voting rights as necessary to the survival of their party. Others liked the idea because they hoped a constitutional amendment would protect African-American voting rights in the South sufficiently that it would no longer be necessary to maintain federal troops there. (Since the passage of the Reconstruction Act, federal troops had been stationed in the South to ensure that the civil rights of the newly freed slaves—including the right to vote—were not compromised.) But not all who supported a Fifteenth Amendment had such a practical rationale for their position. Many lawmakers supported the idea as a matter of principle. Quite a few took political risks in making their views known.

Debates Over the Vote

From December 1868 to February 1869, all aspects of African-American voting rights were debated. Questions such as whether voting was a right or a privilege, whether the right to vote should be controlled by the state or federal government, whether or not suffrage should be universal, and whether voting rights should be protected by an act of Congress or a constitutional amendment were all discussed.

National lawmakers took up the issue when the

third session of the fortieth Congress convened in January 1869. The question of a Fifteenth Amendment was viewed as the most important item on the agenda. It took up nearly the entire session. Debates on the issue were long, complex, and heated. The Senate and the House frequently met until the wee hours of the morning, locked in discussion. When the *Congressional Globe* published these debates, they ran to three hundred pages.[17]

In order to amend, or change, the Constitution, a two-thirds majority vote on the proposed amendment is required in both the Senate and the House of Representatives. Then the amendment must be ratified by three quarters of the states. A number of different versions of a new Fifteenth Amendment were proposed early on. The first to be passed in the House was one proposed by Representative George Boutwell of Massachusetts. It read in part, "The right of any citizen of the United States to vote shall not be denied or abridged by the United States or any State by reason of race, color, or previous condition of slavery of any citizen or class of citizens of the United States."[18] After being approved by two thirds of the House on January 30, 1869, Boutwell's amendment went to the Senate for consideration.

In the Senate, it was subjected to very close and critical scrutiny. Opinions varied greatly. Fifteen substitute versions were proposed in the course of the debates. The dominant reaction, however, was that Boutwell's amendment did not go far enough. Charles Sumner proposed adding a guarantee of the right to hold office. Sumner, and other Radical Republicans, wanted to leave absolutely no room for discrimination to slip through unchecked. They did not want to see African Americans forbidden to hold public office

Massachusetts Representative George Boutwell proposed the first constitutional amendment that would give African-American men the right to vote. Boutwell's proposal met resistance in the Senate because it failed to grant the right to hold political office.

simply because this right had not been explicitly spelled out in the amendment. "I have warred with Slavery too long, in all its different forms," Sumner declared, "not to be aroused when this old enemy shows its head under an *alias*."[19] Ultimately, the Senate rejected Boutwell's proposed amendment. Instead, it came up with one of its own. This, the work of Senator Henry Wilson, also of Massachusetts, read:

> No discrimination shall be made in any State among the citizens of the United States in the exercise of the elective franchise or in the right to hold office in any State, on account of race, color, nativity, property, education or religious creed.[20]

It was much more ambitious than Boutwell's, both with respect to which rights, specifically, were covered (office holding as well as voting) and with respect to who was protected.

It could be predicted that Wilson's amendment would not win sufficient support in the House. For one thing, many northern states had voting requirements that they were not about to give up. Wilson's amendment would have outlawed these requirements. Connecticut and Massachusetts, for example, both had literacy requirements. In Rhode Island, foreign-born voters had to prove they owned real estate worth a certain amount. These all would have been outlawed by the Senate proposal. On February 15, the House officially took up Wilson's proposed amendment for debate. After seeming to be deadlocked, the House finally voted to defeat it. In a surprising move, the stalemate had been broken by the old abolitionist leader Wendell Phillips. Phillips would have liked to see a guarantee of African-American office holding in the amendment. He believed, however, that anything stronger than Boutwell's original proposal would

Massachusetts Senator Henry Wilson was in favor of an amendment that comprehensively guaranteed the right to vote and hold office to all males, regardless of their race, religion, education, or economic status.

never be ratified by three quarters of the states. Boutwell's amendment, he said, covered "all the ground that the people are ready to occupy. [F]or the first time in our lives," he urged, "we beseech them [congressmen, especially the more radical ones] to be a little more *politicians*—and a little less reformers. . . ."[21]

The Fifteenth Amendment Emerges

After voting to defeat the Senate's Wilson Amendment, the House requested a conference committee. The committee would be composed of members of both the House and the Senate. Its job would be to try to iron out the differences between the two houses of Congress. The Senate, however, refused. Two days later, on February 17, the senators began to reconsider an earlier proposal by William Stewart of Nevada. The debate that day on Stewart's amendment lasted twelve hours. Some senators seemed willing to go along with it. Others refused to budge. One frustrated senator, William Fessenden, declared that the Republican Party was "so cut up and divided, and there are so many opinions among the members composing it" that a two-thirds majority vote could not be won for any proposal.[22] Finally, Senator Oliver Morton of Indiana begged his fellow members of the Senate to stop arguing and start acting. He warned them that every day eaten up by debates meant one less day for the states to ratify. He urged them to take half a loaf if they could not get a whole one. At the end of the day, February 17, the Senate at last voted to accept Stewart's proposal. It contained wording very close to that of the Fifteenth Amendment we know today. The fight was still far from over, however.

On February 20, the House considered the Stewart

Nevada Senator William Stewart was responsible for the version of the Fifteenth Amendment that was ultimately approved and added to the Constitution.

Amendment. It approved a revised version. This new version added "nativity, property and creed" to the list of unacceptable reasons for denying the vote. The Senate predictably rejected the House's revised version. Again a conference was asked for, but this time the request was approved by both houses. Finally, on February 26, with the galleries tense and strained, a roll was called in both houses. The Fifteenth Amendment in its present form was passed, 145 to 44 by the House and 39 to 13 by the Senate. It reads as follows:

> The right of citizens of the United States to vote shall not be denied or abridged by the United States or by any State on account of race, color, or previous condition of servitude.
>
> The Congress shall have the power to enforce this article by appropriate legislation.[23]

The new amendment did not mention the right to hold office. It also did not forbid the use of such requirements for voting as literacy, property, or educational tests—all of which could easily be used to discriminate against African-American voters. Still, the amendment accomplished what it had set out to do: it guaranteed the vote to both southern and northern African Americans. The press was very supportive of the new amendment. The *Independent* called it "a flood-wave that will float the Constitution still further toward the final high-water mark of Liberty, Equality, and Fraternity."[24]

States Review the Fifteenth Amendment

On February 26, 1869, the amendment was officially recommended to the states for their ratification (approval). The six-week battle in Congress had been just the beginning. Now there would be a battle in each of the existing twenty-six states. There were a number of forces working in favor of ratification. Three quarters of the states had voted Republican in 1868. Republicans would be far more likely to vote in favor of the new amendment. In addition, President Grant gave it strong support in his first inaugural address. However, there were also a number of forces working against ratification. For one thing, only ten states were needed to vote against the amendment for it to be defeated. Democrats controlled five of the law-making bodies still in session in March 1869. Also, many Republicans were opposed to the amendment.

The debate took much the same shape throughout the states. The arguments most commonly used in favor of ratification were the following:

1. If African Americans were good enough to fight and die for the Union, they were good enough to vote.

2. African Americans deserved a chance to make it on their own, and the vote would give them that chance.

3. Northern African Americans (the ones primarily affected by the amendment, since under Reconstruction southern blacks were already voting) were more educated and less numerous than their southern brethren. They were thus less likely to cause any trouble at the polls.

4. The amendment would help the Republicans to stay in power.

The arguments most commonly used against ratification were the following:

1. The amendment was unconstitutional. It created new federal powers and deprived the states of their

constitutional right to regulate elections and set qualifications for voting.

2. African Americans should not vote because they were illiterate and in other ways inferior to whites.

3. Allowing African Americans to vote would lead to interracial marriage and race wars.[25]

In each region, however, the debate had its own distinctive features. Most New England states ratified the amendment with few problems. Surprisingly, the southern states could also, for the most part, be counted on to ratify. This was because, under Reconstruction, African Americans in the South had already been given the vote. The amendment would result in no great change. Also, southerners opposed to African Americans voting realized that they could still use literacy, property, and poll tax (voting tax) requirements to disqualify many potential African-American voters. The *Daily Richmond Whig* noted that the amendment had "loopholes through which a coach and four horses can be driven."[26] In southern states where the vote appeared to be close, Senator Oliver Morton used his influence to win approval. He did much to help ensure ratification in Texas, Mississippi, Virginia, and Georgia.

On the Pacific Coast, an obstacle to ratification was presented by the question of Chinese voters. If passed, the new amendment would allow the West's large numbers of Chinese immigrants, as well as African Americans, to vote. Many westerners were violently opposed to this idea. Of the far western states, only Nevada approved the amendment.

The border states—Maryland, Kentucky, Delaware, West Virginia, and Missouri—were in general fiercely opposed to ratification. They were staunchly

Indiana Senator Oliver Morton used his considerable influence to help win approval of the Fifteenth Amendment in the southern states whose lawmakers were evenly divided on the issue.

Democratic and opposed to African-American voting. In these states, even Republicans who were in favor of the amendment were afraid to make their views known.

The closest contest was in the Midwest and in the mid-Atlantic states. In these states, an African-American voting bloc would represent a critical swing vote. This could make the difference between a Republican and a Democratic victory in future elections. Both parties were keenly aware of this fact. Ratification was won in Indiana, Illinois, and Ohio.

By the end of March 1869, the required three quarters of the states had voted in favor of the amendment, and it became law. A one-hundred-gun salute was fired in Washington, D.C. Across the country, huge rallies were held and fireworks were set off. Editors wrote flowery tributes to the new amendment. *The New York Times,* for example, called it "the final crowning of the edifice of republicanism."[27] President Grant sent the following special message to the nation:

> A measure which makes at once four millions of people voters, who were heretofore declared by the highest tribunal in the land not citizens of the United States, nor eligible to become so . . . is indeed a measure of grander importance than any other one act of the kind from the foundation of our free government to the present day.[28]

William Lloyd Garrison, founder of the American Anti-Slavery Society, declared that "nothing in all history [equals] this wonderful, quiet, sudden transformation of four millions of human beings from . . . the auction block to the ballot box."[29] In fact, Garrison found the new amendment so significant that in May 1869 he dissolved the society. The passage of the Fifteenth Amendment represented the fulfillment of its pledge to African Americans.

Despite all of the moving and eloquent statements, the outlook for the future of African Americans and their access to the ballot box was not nearly as rosy as it seemed. One of the first signs that trouble lay ahead came the year after the Fifteenth Amendment was passed. In May 1870, Congress passed the first Force Act. This was an act that provided for the supervision of elections by means of federal force. The law spelled out dozens of types of interference with the civil and political rights of African Americans that would from then on be considered crimes. Clearly, strong resistance to the new amendment was anticipated.

A Short-Lived Victory

"The Fifteenth Amendment confers upon the African race the care of its own destiny. It places their fortunes in their own hands."[1] This remark, by Congressman James Garfield, was typical of the thinking of many northerners shortly after the passage of the amendment giving the vote to African Americans. The "negro question," as it was often called, had been a major cause of the Civil War. The country was growing rapidly, business and industry were moving in bold new directions, and many people were eager to turn their attention to other matters. They sought to justify their increasing impatience with issues concerning fair treatment for African Americans. They claimed that, in granting them the right to vote, they had given African Americans all the means they needed to take care of such matters themselves.

Such a claim could scarcely have been further from the truth. Many changes had taken place with respect to the position of African Americans in the South. Still, the attitudes of the majority of white southerners toward African Americans had changed very little. Most were convinced African Americans were incapable of functioning as citizens, even though they now had this status. The election of African-American senators and congressmen had not helped most white southerners learn to accept or respect African-American political activity. Instead, it made them resent politically active African Americans more fiercely than ever. The lawmakers in most southern states had passed laws forbidding discrimination against African Americans. These laws, however, were openly and regularly defied. African Americans were regularly denied the use of railroad cars, hotels, and other public facilities that whites had access to.

Limits on the Right to Vote

Very shortly after the Fifteenth Amendment was passed, Democrats in several states developed clever ways to limit the African-American vote. In 1870, Tennessee amended its constitution to require the payment of a poll tax in order to vote. That same year, Maryland enacted a property qualification for voting. In Virginia, lawmakers gerrymandered (established the borders of electoral districts to benefit one political party) the cities in order to ensure Democratic control of these local governments. The state also reduced the number of polling places in African-American precincts and passed its own poll tax.

Violence Increases

These attempts at restricting African-American voters were supplemented by other methods that were far less legal. Violence against African Americans had been commonplace throughout Reconstruction. However, as the decade of the 1860s progressed, it increased dramatically. Militias (private military groups) had been banned in the South under Reconstruction. Southerners easily found a way around such restrictions, however. They formed volunteer fire companies and rifle clubs that were, in effect, quasimilitary organizations. Their purpose was to intimidate African Americans. If they were ordered to disband, they simply reorganized as dancing clubs or missionary societies.

In 1865, a secret society called the Ku Klux Klan was founded in Tennessee. The group's name was derived from the Greek word for circle, kuklos.[2] Its founders described the Ku Klux Klan as "an institution of chivalry, humanity, mercy and patriotism."[3] Its aim, however, was to kill or drive away leading blacks and the whites who helped them. Wearing white robes as a disguise (claiming to be the ghosts of dead Confederate soldiers), Klansmen brutalized, terrorized, and murdered thousands of southern blacks and whites sympathetic to their cause. The entries that follow are just a fraction of those in a list of such incidents compiled by Kentucky African Americans. Many others were also compiled as part of a petition to the governor to do something about the problem of Klan violence.

- School house for African Americans burned by incendiaries in Breckinridge, December 24, 1867.

- Jim Macklin, an African American, is taken from jail in Frankfort and hung by mob, January 28, 1868.

- Sam Davis hung by mob in Harrodsburg, May 28, 1868.

- William Pierce hung by a mob in Christian, July 12, 1868.

- George Roger hung by a mob in Bradsfordville, Martin County, July 11, 1868.

- School Exhibition at Midway attacked by a mob, July 31, 1868.

- Silas Woodford, age sixty, badly beaten by disguised mob. Mary Smith Curtis and Margaret Mosby also badly beaten, near Keene, Jessemine County, August 1868.

- Caleb Fields shot and killed by disguised men near Keene, Jessamine County, August 3, 1868.

- James Gaines expelled from Anderson by Ku Klux Klan, August 1868.

- James Parker killed by Ku Klux Klan in Pulaski, August 1868.[4]

Ku Klux Klan Activity

Klansmen frequently included the most respectable members of white southern society—planters, merchants, lawyers, even ministers. Their victims included African Americans from all walks of life. Those involved in holding a political office were the most at risk. Charles Caldwell was an African-American state senator from Mississippi. He "was lured into a cellar, shot numerous times, then carried into the street where his body was 'grotesquely turned completely over by the impact of innumerable shots fired at close range.'"[5] Joseph Rainey, an African-American congressman from South Carolina, received a letter from the Klan that said, in red ink, "K.K.K. Beware! Beware! Beware! Your doom is sealed in blood."[6] But the Klan also took a special disliking to ordinary African Americans whom they considered overeducated or in some other way "uppity." The

Wearing hoods and robes to protect their identities, members of the Ku Klux Klan used brutal tactics to prevent African Americans from voting and from having any real place in society at all.

brother of an African-American man from Georgia was murdered by the Klan. He said his brother had been a target because he was "too big a man . . . he can write and read and put it down himself."[7]

The Klan also made regular targets of African-American schools and churches. They regularly burned schools and whipped, tortured, and murdered schoolteachers. Klan activity was so intense in some regions that many African Americans regularly slept in the woods to escape harm.[8] The total number of blacks killed by the Klan during the Reconstruction Era is estimated to be between twenty thousand and forty thousand.[9] Countless others were cruelly whipped or beaten, and hundreds of homes, schools, and churches were destroyed.

For a short period, the federal government did take steps to combat such atrocities. Violence such as that perpetrated by Klansmen helped persuade Congress to pass the Force Acts of 1870, 1871, and 1872. It was clear, at least to some lawmakers, that in order for African Americans to be able to exercise the rights guaranteed them by the Fifteenth Amendment, the force of the federal government would be needed. The last of the Force Acts, also known as the Ku Klux Klan Act, gave federal troops special powers to combat Klan activities. It set forth heavy penalties for conspirators. It also allowed the president to suspend the writ of *habeas corpus* (a legal safeguard that prevents authorities from holding a person in custody without due cause). For a while, the national government conducted a vigorous attack on the Klan. In upcountry South Carolina, President Grant sent in federal troops and had hundreds arrested. Elsewhere, hundreds were indicted (formally charged by the courts with a crime).

By 1872, there had been a dramatic decrease in Klan violence.

Standing up to white southern resistance to African-American civil rights was no easy task, however. Federal election supervisors, whose presence in the South was authorized by the Enforcement Acts, were badly harassed. Many of the indictments of Klansmen only led to suspended sentences in southern courts. Those accused and those called as witnesses used such excuses as "short memories," or "illness of defendants" to destroy the government's cases.[10] It was not long before the government grew tired of requests for intervention. By 1873, it was doing little to enforce the Ku Klux Klan Act. By 1874, it had stopped enforcing the act almost entirely.

In the late 1860s and early 1870s, local political parties whose members called themselves "Conservatives" had sprung up all over the South. Klan violence did much to help bring the new parties and the old southern Democrats to power. In Oglethorpe County, Georgia, for example, Republicans received eleven hundred votes in the March 1868 elections. Eight months later, in the November election, the Republicans received only 116 votes. The dramatic difference between the two figures was a result of Klan activity between the elections.[11]

Charges of corruption on the part of African-American politicians helped bring over more southern Republicans—even though many of the charges were unsubstantiated. (One Mississippi historian who, around the turn of the century, did a study of his state at the time of Reconstruction found that only two charges of theft on the part of Reconstruction politicians could be verified. In one case, a black man stole books from a public library; in another, a white man stole seven thousand dollars from the state.)[12] Democrats also frequently used intimidation in order to secure victories for members of their party at the polls.

The story of Mississippi's bloody and lawless transition from a Republican to a Democratic state is a typical one. In the 1874 elections, a White Man's Party was organized in Vicksburg. The party used armed gangs to patrol the streets and intimidate African Americans into staying at home and not going out to vote. In the countryside, White Leagues were organized. These leagues demanded that a black sheriff resign, and armed bands roamed the area, killing about three hundred blacks. Eventually, the federal government intervened and restored the sheriff to office.[13]

By 1875, however, the government had grown tired of requests for help around election time. That year, Democratic rifle clubs disrupted Republican meetings and assaulted local Republican leaders. Roaming bands of armed whites killed hundreds of blacks suspected of Republican sympathies. On the eve of Election Day, armed riders rode around threatening to kill African Americans if they showed up to vote. In one community, cannons and cavalry were lined up around the polling places to prevent African Americans from gaining access to them. Elsewhere, they guarded the fords across the rivers African Americans needed to cross in order to reach the election sites. Finally, Mississippi governor Adelbert Ames asked President Grant for federal troops to help keep order and stop the killings. The attorney general refused the request. Many areas reported overwhelming Democratic victories. In Yazoo County, only seven Republican votes were counted in 1875; there had been twenty-five hundred in 1874.[14] In places where Republicans did manage to win, the violence continued. Newly elected officials were forced to resign under threat of death. Even Governor Ames was forced to resign or be impeached.

Democrats Gain Control

By the end of 1874, Democrats had gained control of the governments of Texas, Arkansas, Mississippi, and Alabama. North Carolina, Virginia, and Georgia were already Conservative. The other southern states would soon follow suit. Even among Republicans, support for protecting the rights of African Americans was decreasing. New Republican leaders were less idealistic than those that had come before them. Their chief concern was simply to keep their party in power. In 1875, Congress passed the last civil rights act for nearly one hundred years. The act forbade discrimination on the basis of race in hotels, railroads, restaurants, and other places of public accommodation. No effort was made to enforce the act, however, and a few years later the Supreme Court declared it unconstitutional. By 1876, both the Republican presidential candidate, Rutherford B. Hayes, and Democrat Samuel Tilden, promised voters they would end Reconstruction. Shortly after he was elected, President Hayes made good on his promise. He withdrew the last of the federal troops from the South. Reconstruction was officially over. So, too, for the most part, were voting rights for African Americans.

During the last years of the 1870s, the government followed the pullout of the federal troops authorized under Reconstruction with a withdrawal of the federal troops. Officials who had been used to ensure that African Americans were able to exercise their Fifteenth Amendment rights also left. In 1878, the use of the Army at elections was forbidden. The Justice Department also retreated dramatically from its efforts to prosecute those who interfered with African Americans who wanted to vote. Between 1870 and 1877, the department prosecuted an average of seven hundred cases a year of voting irregularities in the South. The conviction rate at the beginning of that period was 74 percent. By the end, it was only 10 percent. By 1878, after federal troops were forbidden to assist at elections, only twenty-five voting rights cases were even brought to trial.[15]

The retreat on the part of the Justice Department was fueled by two Supreme Court decisions. These cases did much to prevent prosecution of those who interfered with African-American voting rights. The Fifteenth Amendment had said that no *state* could deny or abridge the right of the citizens to vote. However, it said nothing about what private individuals could or could not do. In two 1876 cases, *United States* v. *Cruikshank* and *United States* v. *Reese,* the Supreme Court said that the federal government could not punish violations of the Enforcement Acts on the part of private individuals. It could only correct official state actions that denied blacks their civil rights. In *United States* v. *Reese,* the Court established that the Fifteenth Amendment had not granted African Americans the right to vote. It had merely prohibited the states from denying suffrage on racial grounds. In short, these two decisions said that most of the attempts southerners had made to keep African Americans from voting were legally justified.

Intimidation Continues

Without now having to worry about federal interference, white southerners continued to prevent (by means of intimidation, violence, and fraud) blacks from voting. They set up polling places that were especially far from the areas where African Americans lived. The ferries that African Americans had to use to get to polling places mysteriously went "out of repair" right around Election Day. The locations of polling places were changed without the African-American community being told. Those who did manage to make it to the polls were confronted with elaborate and confusing balloting processes. In South Carolina, for example, voters had to use eight separate ballot boxes, a separate one for each office. If a voter put a ballot in the wrong box, it was not counted.[16]

The vote was being put steadily further and further out of the reach of most southern African Americans. At the same time, their other recently won rights were also being withdrawn. Laws known as "Jim Crow" laws began to be passed in all the southern states. Jim Crow laws enforced the separation of the races in such public places as railroads, streetcars, depots, waiting rooms, theaters, hotels, barbershops, and restaurants. Facilities for blacks were universally inferior to their white counterparts.

Yet, despite this steady retreat from the guarantees of the Fourteenth and Fifteenth Amendments, some African Americans did continue to vote. Until the 1890s, they were occasionally even able to elect some of their own people to office. The survival of this small bit of African-American political power was made possible in large part because of class divisions among southern whites. In order to gain a victory for their own candidate, these groups would take turns courting the black vote. The black voters and politicians who survived during these years developed considerable political skills. An Englishman named George Campbell visited the South in 1879. He delivered a glowing report of what he observed on his travels:

> During the last dozen years the Negroes have had a very large share of political education. Considering the troubles and the ups and downs that they have gone through, it is, I think, wonderful how beneficial this education has been to them, and how much these people, so lately in the most debased condition of slavery, have acquired independent ideas; and, far from lapsing into anarchy, have become citizens with ideas of law and property and order. The white serfs of Europe took hundreds of years to rise to the level which these Negroes adopted in America.[17]

Undermining the Fifteenth Amendment

The 1890s, however, were to witness the near-total eclipse of African-American political activity in the South. In 1890, Senator Henry Cabot Lodge of Massachusetts proposed a bill to institute federal supervision of national elections. It did not pass. The mere fact of its being proposed scared southern whites, however. Poor farmers and wealthy planters forgot their differences and closed ranks to work together to disenfranchise (take the vote away from) African Americans. Across the South, there was agreement that some legal way must be found to deny African Americans the vote without violating the Fifteenth Amendment. This also had to be done without at the same time affecting poor and illiterate whites.

The state of Mississippi was the first to come up with a solution. In 1890, the state called a convention to draft a new constitution. Delegates were quite open about why they had assembled. They were there to find a way to suppress the African-American vote. "If you fail in the discharge of your duties in this matter," said Judge S. S. Calhoun, "the blood of every negro that will be killed in an election riot hereafter will be upon your shoulders."[18] In other words, if the convention failed to come up with a legal means of keeping African Americans from voting, the old tactics of intimidation and violence would continue. A plan was eventually proposed and agreed upon. Under the plan, anyone who wanted to vote or register to vote and who could not meet a stiff property-owning qualification would have to present satisfactory evidence either of good character or of three to five years of steady employment. Otherwise, he would have to prove he could read and write and understand the federal Constitution. This understanding would be tested by reading aloud any section of the Constitution. The potential voter would then be asked to give a reasonable interpretation of it. Whether or not his answer was reasonable would, of course, be determined by the person conducting the examination. This would make it easy to rule against blacks and in favor of whites without the use of any obviously discriminatory laws. The new constitution also required that voters register months before an election. Anyone who wanted to register had to show a receipt proving that he had paid his taxes (a stipulation designed to trip up African Americans, who were not used to saving documents). Voters also had to pay a poll tax. The voting requirements of the new state constitution were tested in the Supreme Court in the case of *Williams* v. *Mississippi*. They were found not to be in violation of the federal Constitution.

The other southern states quickly followed in Mississippi's footsteps. One after another they held conventions and drafted new state constitutions. Between 1890 and 1908, eight southern states passed new constitutions or amended their old ones. In addition to the methods described above, a number of the new constitutions included what were known as "grandfather clauses." These allowed the passage of strict new voting requirements while protecting white citizens from their restrictions. Grandfather clauses guaranteed permanent voter registration, without their having to meet any other requirements, to all who had been able to vote prior to 1861 and to their descendants. Anyone who had served in the Confederate or Union Army and their descendants were also allowed to vote. Almost all white southerners fell into one of these categories. Almost no blacks did, as they had been enslaved prior to 1861. The delegates were unabashed in stating what they were about. "Discrimination! Why, that is precisely what we propose," said Carter Glass of Virginia, later elected a U.S. senator from that state. "That, exactly, is what this convention was elected for—to discriminate to the very extremity of permissible action . . . with a view to the elimination of every Negro voter who can be gotten rid of, legally. . . ."[19]

The success of the new state constitutions in accomplishing their admitted purpose was unquestionable. In Louisiana, for example, 130,344 African Americans registered to vote in the election of 1896, before the drafting of the new constitution. By the election of 1904, several years after the new constitution was approved, only 1,324 African Americans registered.[20]

At the turn of the century, the political situation of southern African Americans was nearly as bad as it had been in pre-Civil War times. In some ways, it was

Booker T. Washington was an advocate for education and
advancement of African Americans. Like many other leaders
though, he said little about voting rights, implying that
politics were not a matter for African Americans to be
concerned with.

worse. Many African-American leaders, instead of raising a protest as the old abolitionists had, were advising African Americans to accept the new status quo. Booker T. Washington was one of the most prominent African-American leaders at the turn of the century. He did little to speak out against the new southern constitutions. Instead, he advised his people to concentrate on achieving economic independence and not to concern themselves with politics. With African Americans having almost no access to the ballot box, and no leaders encouraging people to fight for such access, the future of their voting rights looked dim indeed.

A Right
Regained

In the first decades of the twentieth century, a wide variety of factors came together to make African-American voting in the South all but obsolete. The restrictions set up by the new southern state constitutions, of course, did much to disqualify many would-be African-American voters. There were, however, a number of other factors operating as well. One was the rise of the all-white primary system. All-white primaries had their origins back in Reconstruction. A primary is an election held by a political party to enable members of that party to choose a candidate. It is not technically considered an official state or federal election. Therefore, it was not covered by the Fifteenth Amendment. Southerners took advantage of this situation to overtly restrict voting in primaries to whites. After 1876, the Democrats virtually controlled southern politics. This ensured that African Americans would have almost no chance of ever being able to nominate and vote for either a black or a white candidate sympathetic to their situation. All Democratic candidates were nominated in white-only primary elections.

Problems at the Polls

Another factor that kept even "qualified" African Americans from voting was the humiliating treatment they regularly received at the polls. Many complained that they were ridiculed, or told the "quota" for African-American voters had been filled. Many were simply refused entry for no reason. The position of Governor Vardaman of Mississippi on African-American voting was typical of southern whites in the early years of the twentieth century. "I am opposed to Negro voting . . . it matters not what his advertised moral and mental qualifications may be."[1] African-American voters were also harassed by the mere process of registering. In most southern states, in order to register to vote you had to provide ten or more personal details. Would-be voters were often required to provide these "without aid, suggestion, or memorandum" (in other words, on a blank piece of paper). White voters were often given hints, or were even given a sheet listing the required information. African-American voters, on the other hand, were given no such help.[2]

Still another factor that kept many African Americans home on Election Day was the political indifference that had become widespread among African Americans in the South. The slow unraveling of the dreams that had been born in many African Americans after the Civil War had left many demoralized and politically apathetic. "Politics is the white folks' business" was a common attitude, even among well-educated African Americans. "As a group we are sleeping," lamented an African-American doctor from Norfolk, Virginia.[3]

But just when the political future of African Americans looked dimmest, a movement began that would eventually rekindle people's hopes. Around the turn of the century, W.E.B. Du Bois and other northern African-American professionals began a movement dedicated to fighting for voting rights for African Americans. They argued that the right to vote was necessary if African Americans were to advance themselves in any way. "No improvement in the economic and social condition of Negroes is going to be made so long as they are deprived of political power to support and defend it," Du Bois said.[4] The vote was the first step in liberating southern African Americans from the discrimination and injustice to which they were subjected in all areas of their lives. It was also an integral part of being a citizen. Gradually, northern whites also began to take an interest in the new movement. In 1910, the movement became an official organization called the National Association for the Advancement of Colored People (NAACP). It was dedicated to promoting racial equality and justice.

The NAACP Steps In

The NAACP began its fight for voting rights for African Americans in the courts. In 1915, the Supreme Court declared grandfather clauses unconstitutional. By 1916, the Court had ruled against other clever regulations aimed at preventing African Americans from voting. Justice Felix Frankfurter was strong in his defense of the guarantees of the Fifteenth Amendment. He said, "The [Fifteenth] Amendment nullifies sophisticated as well as simpleminded modes of discrimination. It hits onerous [burdensome] procedural requirements which effectively handicap exercise of the franchise [right to vote] by the colored race although the abstract right to vote may remain unrestricted as to face."[5]

A Gradual Increase in Voters

By the 1920s, the number of African Americans voting was gradually beginning to increase. This was due to several factors. First, there was an increase in the number of "open elections." These were elections held outside the white primary system. This was especially true in cities. Cities began to hold referendum votes on various issues. (A referendum is a proposed law that is submitted to the people for approval.) There could be no primary in such cases. Also, cities with city manager-type governments or with commission-type governments (as opposed to governments headed by a mayor) generally did not hold primaries for their municipal elections. By 1927, 115 southern cities had city manager governments and thirty-two had commission governments.[6] There were other reasons for a rise in African-American votes in cities as well. Those who lived in cities formed their own social and civic groups. It was more difficult to refuse to let someone vote who was visibly active in the community. It was also easier for people who lived in cities to organize politically. Gradually, African-American political leaders began to emerge. Finally, cities tended to attract better educated and more prosperous people, both black and white. Educated and financially successful African Americans were more likely to push to vote. Well-educated urban whites tended to be somewhat less prejudiced than rural southern whites. They were more inclined to favor black voting rights.

By 1928, African-American votes were beginning

to make a difference in national elections. In the presidential race of that year, the white southern vote was fairly evenly divided between Herbert Hoover (Republican) and Al Smith (Democrat). Both parties thus courted southern African-American voters. In 1928, most African Americans were still voting Republican, and Herbert Hoover was able to win the election. However, despite the steps forward that had been made, the African-American vote was still woefully small. In 1930, the largest number of African Americans to register in a southern state was only some eighteen thousand, in Virginia. This represented only 5.2 percent of the literate African-American population of voting age in the state.[7] A vicious cycle was at work helping to keep the percentage of African Americans voting down. A low African-American voter turnout meant there would be less incentive for other African Americans to vote. It also meant that whites would be more inclined to disregard their demands and needs. This disregard on the part of whites further discouraged blacks from voting. The small number of African-American voters also discouraged those African Americans who might have considered becoming political leaders.

In the 1930s, national economic changes and population changes meant that more African Americans than ever were able to vote. Large numbers of African Americans had moved to northern cities. Voting was much easier there. African-American farmers in the South also got opportunities to vote under President Franklin Roosevelt's New Deal. It included an agricultural program, which began in 1938. Tenant farmers and sharecroppers were given the right to vote on yearly crop-restriction issues. For many African-American farmers, this was their first taste of what it felt like to cast a ballot.

More Legal Battles

African Americans continued to work to have legal obstacles to their votes removed through the court system. Their first target was the white primary system. At first, the Justice Department was reluctant to pursue the matter. Perhaps it feared alienating white southern Democrats. Roosevelt's was a Democratic administration. It was dependent on the support of southern Democrats to remain in power. By April 3, 1944, however, the Supreme Court had ruled that primaries were an integral part of the election machinery and African Americans could not be prevented from voting in them.

Shortly thereafter, African-American servicemen returned home from overseas duty in World War II. The new veterans were more in earnest than ever about voting. It is estimated that, in 1932, one hundred thousand African Americans had been registered to vote in the South. By 1947, the total had reached almost six hundred fifty thousand.[8] In the 1948 presidential election, African-American voters played a decisive role in Harry Truman's victory. They were able to swing the important states of California, Illinois, and Ohio to the Democrats.[9]

President Truman, in turn, supported the use of federal power to win voting rights for African Americans. In 1946, he sent a greeting to the NAACP in support of their efforts. In it, he said that the "ballot is both a right and a privilege . . . [the] right to use it must be protected and its use by everyone must be encouraged."[10]

With the white primary struck down, the next

major obstacle to African-American voting was the poll tax. The poll tax was attacked steadily throughout the 1940s and 1950s. A 1942 Gallup poll showed that 63 percent of Americans wanted to see the poll tax repealed.[11] Efforts by Congress to do away with the tax were vigorously opposed by southern congressmen. However, by the 1950s, despite the southern defense, several states had either reduced the tax or done away with it altogether.

Progress was being made, but the pace was painfully slow. Even by the mid-1950s, there were still thousands of African Americans of voting age in the South—more than 75 percent of them, in fact—who were not even registered.[12] Something more effective than court and legal battles clearly was needed if African Americans were ever to fully claim the rights promised them in the Fifteenth Amendment.

In 1946, two African-American brothers had recently come home from serving their country overseas. They went to vote in their hometown of Decatur, Mississippi. One of the brothers recalled what happened that day:

> When we arrived at the courthouse, there must have been two hundred rednecks, dressed in overalls and holding their shotguns. . . . They were sitting around in their pickup trucks and standing over the courthouse square. When we tried to go into the courthouse they blocked the doors and refused to let us through. . . . Then the ol' circuit clerk, Mr. Brand, came around saying, "Charles, you and Medgar, you all go back, you gonna cause trouble."
>
> And I said, "Let me tell you something, Mr. Brand. We are going to vote. . . . It's up to you. *Give us our ballot.*" . . . When we tried to get in the side door and the front door, they were blocked. The druggist, Andy Mays, was blocking one door, and when we tried to walk in he said, "Listen . . . ain't nothin' happened to you yet."

> I . . . flashed my switchblade knife at him and he stepped back and Medgar and I walked through. . . .
>
> We were inside the courthouse. We had received our ballots to vote, but there wasn't any way we could get to the ballot box, because the Klansmen had put the ballot box *inside* a back office and they were physically blocking the door to that office. . . .
>
> I really wanted to die that day.[13]

Eventually, the two brothers were able to cast their votes. The painful and humiliating experience they underwent simply trying to do their civic duty helped inspire the two men. They got involved in a new movement to win full and permanent equality for African Americans. The men were Medgar and Charles Evers. Both went on to become leaders of one of the greatest grassroots movements this country has ever seen—the Civil Rights Movement of the 1950s and 1960s.

Important Victories

By the mid-1950s, the Civil Rights Movement had achieved several outstanding victories. One of them was the Supreme Court's 1954 *Brown* v. *Board of Education*. This decision made segregated schools illegal. Another was the Montgomery (Alabama) bus boycott, in which a brave African-American woman named Rosa Parks helped lead a successful fight for the right to sit in any empty seat on a city bus. But as progress was made on other fronts, southern white resistance to black voting did not wane; rather, it increased. In Macon County, Alabama, for example, there were 3,081 whites of voting age in 1958 and 14,539 African Americans of voting age. Yet, the books show that 3,102 whites were registered to vote that year, while only 1,218 blacks were registered.[14]

In the 1950s, a massive campaign to register

During the 1950s and 1960s, African Americans became much more active in their quest for civil rights. Seeking enforcement of the rights guaranteed to them by the Constitution, hundreds of thousands of African Americans marched in Washington, D.C.

southern African-American voters was undertaken. From the outset, those involved in the campaign had to confront hostility that frequently escalated to the point of violence. In May 1955, Reverend George Lee from Belzoni, Mississippi, was shot in the face with a shotgun and killed after he became the first African American in the city to register to vote. The police ruled his death a traffic accident.[15] Lamar Smith, an African American, had voted in Mississippi's Democratic primary. On August 13, 1955, he was shot to death in broad daylight in front of the Brookhaven (Mississippi) courthouse. No arrests were made.[16] It was evident those working to register African-American voters in the South would need some kind of federal protection.

In 1957, the nation's first civil rights bill in almost one hundred years was passed. The bill dealt primarily with voting rights. But the government dragged its heels setting up the guidelines and staff needed to enforce the new law. The Justice Department was extremely cautious in its enforcement of the law. It prosecuted only the most flagrant violations. Few African-American voters were registered as a result of the 1957 civil rights bill.

In the 1960s, the fight for civil rights for African Americans took on a new intensity. When John F. Kennedy was elected President, he obtained funding for massive southern voter registration drives. The Civil Rights Division of the Justice Department became more active in supporting those who faced discrimination in their attempts to register. Many private civil rights groups soon joined the government in its effort to get out the vote. In 1962, the Voter Education Project began to conduct voter registration campaigns across the South. They were helped by the Student

Nonviolent Coordinating Committee (SNCC), the Southern Christian Leadership Conference (SCLC), and others.

The men and women who tried to register southern African Americans in the early 1960s, as in earlier years, met with extreme hostility. Greenwood, Mississippi, was the scene of some of the most notorious and violent resistance. Those conducting the campaign in Greenwood had their office ransacked, were beaten, and had police threaten to bash in their teeth. Finally, two of their leaders, Robert Moses and Randolph Blackwell, were shot by night riders the night after their most successful day canvassing. Later, the group's headquarters was set on fire.

Despite the hardships they endured, many of those involved, both white and black, found their experiences moving, and even life-changing. Fannie Lou Hamer was the youngest of twenty children of a Mississippi sharecropper family. She had traveled twenty-six miles to try to register to vote. For her efforts, she was fired from her job of eighteen years as timekeeper on a plantation. A man came to tell her, "We are not ready for this in Mississippi," he said. Mrs. Hamer replied, "I didn't register for you, I tried to register for myself."[17] Fannie Lou Hamer went on to become a leader of the SNCC. She helped hundreds of her fellow African Americans register to vote.

Government Assistance

The voter-registration drives of the early 1960s in Mississippi, Louisiana, and Georgia produced disappointing results in terms of numbers. Civil rights activists began to implore the government to come to their aid. At first, President Kennedy resisted asking Congress to pass new laws that would lend support to the registration drives. He feared losing the support of southern Democrats. He needed their votes for other laws. Instead, he pushed for a constitutional amendment abolishing the poll tax, and urged the courts to be more aggressive in prosecuting violations of the earlier civil rights act. When it became clear that neither of these measures would be sufficient, President Kennedy did begin to push for a stronger law. He was killed, however, before it could be passed. Kennedy's successor was Lyndon Johnson. President Johnson had a deep sense of outrage at the indignity people suffered because of discrimination, and a firm commitment to the cause of civil rights. While he was vice president, he remarked to a Mississippi senator:

> The other day a sad thing happened. Helen Williams and her husband, Gene, who have been working for me for many years, drove my official car from Washington down to Texas, the Cadillac limousine of the vice-president of the United States. They drove through your state, and when they got hungry, they stopped at grocery stores on the edge of town in [African-American] areas and bought Vienna sausage and beans and ate them with a plastic spoon. . . . And you know, John, that's just bad. That's wrong. . . . And it seems to me that if people in Mississippi don't change it voluntarily, that it's just going to be necessary to change it by law.[18]

Immediately after assuming the presidency, Johnson turned his attention to getting the Civil Rights Act passed.

On July 2, 1964, the Civil Rights Act was passed. However, the sections that concerned voting rights were the least controversial. They prevented registrars from denying the right to vote because of slight errors or omissions by applicants on their registration papers. (Using complex registration forms and then disqualifying African Americans because of minor errors in filling them out had been a common ploy for keeping southern African Americans from the polls. When one judge reviewed registration documents in Montgomery, Alabama, over a five-year period, he discovered that 1,070 white applicants whose forms contained errors had been accepted by the registrar, while only 54 black applicants with errors in their forms were accepted.)[19]

Attempts to prevent African Americans from registering continued even after passage of the Civil Rights Bill. One graduate of Tuskegee Institute, a southern college for African Americans, complained that while in school she had been asked to copy out Article II of the United States Constitution, which took her eight pages in longhand. She never heard from the board of registrars whether or not her voter registration application had been accepted.[20] This was a typical case. Even the Civil Rights Bill was not strong enough to stop southern communities determined to keep African Americans from voting.

Dr. Martin Luther King, Jr., Steps in

In 1965, Dr. Martin Luther King, Jr., began a series of demonstrations to protest discrimination against would-be African-American voters in Selma, Alabama. The local sheriff had hundreds of demonstrators, including King, arrested. Only then was Dr. King able to confer with President Johnson about the need for new laws. Johnson eventually went to Congress and asked them to pass voting rights laws. "It is not just Negroes, but it is really all of us, who must overcome the crippling legacy of bigotry and injustice," he said. "And we shall overcome."[21]

President Johnson signed the Voting Rights Act on

Dr. Martin Luther King, Jr., was arrested in Selma, Alabama, after protesting the refusal of southern states to allow African Americans to vote.

August 6, 1965—in the same room where Lincoln had signed a bill freeing the slaves owned by Confederates. "Today what is perhaps the last of the legal barriers is tumbling," Johnson said. He called the bill "one of the most monumental laws in the entire history of American freedom."[22] The Voting Rights Act of 1965 did away with literacy tests and all other such voter-application tests. In areas where tests had been used, it allowed federal examiners to enroll qualified people, to ensure fairness.

Within just months of the passage of the new bill, striking results were noted. On August 14, in Selma, 381 African Americans registered to vote. This was more people than the total number who had registered in the previous sixty-five years.[23] Within one year, the percentage of African Americans registered in the South had doubled, climbing to 46 percent.[24] With more people registered, African Americans began to be elected to public office. By 1969, over 120 African Americans held elective office in the five southern states to which federal examiners had been sent.[25] Whites who were openly racist began to be voted out of office. With more blacks (and whites sympathetic to their needs) holding office, the quality of services provided to African-American communities improved noticeably. African-American neighborhoods had more paved streets than they did before, more frequent garbage collection, more African-American police officers on patrol.

Unfortunately, the rapid increase in the number of registered southern African Americans that followed the passage of the Voting Rights Act did not last. By 1969, the percentage of qualified southern African Americans who were registered to vote was still only 60.7 percent. This compared with 83.5 percent of registered southern whites.[26] Various explanations have been given for this leveling off of the number of southern African Americans registered. Some voting rights advocates blamed it on an insufficient number of federal examiners. The Justice Department had not sent examiners to all counties. It claimed that, if a whole army of examiners were sent, they would arouse the hostility of southern whites. But studies showed that the highest registration figures were found in counties to which federal examiners *had* been assigned. Others attributed the lack of continued gain in voting registration among southern African Americans to a lack of political consciousness. Some political scientists say southern African Americans, after so many years of being shut out of the political arena, still tended to think of politics as "white people's business."[27]

Although African Americans have made great strides in reclaiming their political voice, promised them over 125 years ago, there is still progress to be made. In the 1996 elections, African Americans accounted for 10 percent of the votes cast.[28] Twelve percent of the national population is African American, so more people could be voting.[29] Why do problems continue to persist? The answers are only slightly clearer than they were some 125 years ago. Some claim that devious means, such as redrawing voting districts to minimize the impact of African-American votes, are still being used.[30] Others mention ongoing political apathy.[31] Whatever the reason, or reasons, there is still work to be done, by both blacks and whites, to ensure that the vision of equality, participation, and self-determination embodied by the Fifteenth Amendment becomes a reality for all African-American citizens.

THE CONSTITUTION OF THE UNITED STATES

The text of the Constitution is presented here. All words are given their modern spelling and capitalization. Brackets [ ] indicate parts that have been changed or set aside by amendments.

Preamble

We the people of the United States, in order to form a more perfect Union, establish justice, insure domestic tranquility, provide for the common defense, promote the general welfare, and secure the blessings of liberty to ourselves and our posterity, do ordain and establish this Constitution for the United States of America.

ARTICLE I
The Legislative Branch

Section 1. All legislative powers herein granted shall be vested in a Congress of the United States, which shall consist of a Senate and House of Representatives.

The House of Representatives

Section 2. (1) The House of Representatives shall be composed of members chosen every second year by the people of the several states, and the electors in each state shall have the qualifications requisite for electors of the most numerous branch of the state legislature.

(2) No person shall be a representative who shall not have attained the age of twenty-five years, and been seven years a citizen of the United States, and who shall not, when elected, be an inhabitant of that state in which he shall be chosen.

(3) Representatives and direct taxes shall be apportioned among the several states which may be included within this Union, according to their respective numbers, [which shall be determined by adding to the whole number of free persons, including those bound to service for a term of years, and excluding Indians not taxed, three-fifths of all other persons]. The actual enumeration shall be made within three years after the first meeting of the Congress of the United States, and within every subsequent term of ten years, in such manner as they shall by law direct. The number of representatives shall not exceed one for every thirty thousand, but each state shall have at least one representative; [and until such enumeration shall be made, the state of New Hampshire shall be entitled to choose three, Massachusetts eight, Rhode Island and Providence Plantations one, Connecticut five, New York six, New Jersey four, Pennsylvania eight, Delaware one, Maryland six, Virginia ten, North Carolina five, South Carolina five, and Georgia three].

(4) When vacancies happen in the representation from any state, the executive authority thereof shall issue writs of election to fill such vacancies.

(5) The House of Representatives shall choose their Speaker and other officers; and shall have the sole power of impeachment.

The Senate

Section 3. (1) The Senate of the United States shall be composed of two senators from each state, [chosen by the legislature thereof,] for six years; and each senator shall have one vote.

(2) Immediately after they shall be assembled in consequence of the first election, they shall be divided as equally as may be into three classes. The seats of the senators of the first class shall be vacated at the expiration of the second year, of the second class at the expiration of the fourth year, and of the third class at the expiration of the sixth year, so that one-third may be chosen every second year; [and if vacancies happen by resignation, or otherwise, during the recess of the legislature of any state, the executive thereof may make temporary appointments until the next meeting of the legislature, which shall then fill such vacancies].

(3) No person shall be a senator who shall not have attained to the age of thirty years, and been nine years a citizen of the United States, and who shall not, when elected, be an inhabitant of that state for which he shall be chosen.

(4) The Vice President of the United States shall be president of the Senate, but shall have no vote, unless they be equally divided.

(5) The Senate shall choose their other officers, and also a president *pro tempore*, in the absence of the Vice President, or when he shall exercise the office of President of the United States.

(6) The Senate shall have the sole power to try all impeachments. When sitting for that purpose, they shall be on oath or affirmation. When the President of the United States is tried, the Chief Justice shall preside: and no person shall be convicted without the concurrence of two-thirds of the members present.

(7) Judgement in cases of impeachment shall not extend further than to removal from office, and disqualification to hold and enjoy any office of honor, trust, or profit under the United States: but the party convicted shall nevertheless be liable and subject to indictment, trial, judgement and punishment, according to law.

Organization of Congress

Section 4. (1) The times, places and manner of holding elections for senators and representatives, shall be prescribed in each state by the legislature thereof; but the Congress may at any time by law make or alter such regulations, [except as to the places of choosing senators].

(2) The Congress shall assemble at least once in every year, [and such meeting shall be on the first Monday in December], unless they shall by law appoint a different day.

Section 5. (1) Each house shall be the judge of the elections, returns and qualifications of its own members, and a majority of each shall constitute a quorum to do business; but a smaller number may adjourn from day to day, and may be authorized to compel the attendance of absent members, in such manner, and under such penalties as each house may provide.

(2) Each house may determine the rules of its proceedings, punish its members for disorderly behavior, and, with the concurrence of two-thirds, expel a member.

(3) Each house shall keep a journal of its proceedings, and from time to time publish the same, excepting such parts as may in their judgement require secrecy; and the yeas and nays of the members of either house on any question shall, at the desire of one-fifth of those present, be entered on the journal.

(4) Neither house, during the session of Congress, shall, without the consent of the other, adjourn for more than three days, nor to any other place than that in which the two houses shall be sitting.

Section 6. (1) The senators and representatives shall receive a compensation for their services, to be ascertained by law, and paid out of the treasury of the United States. They shall in all cases, except treason, felony and breach of the peace, be privileged from arrest during their attendance at the session of their respective houses, and in going to and returning from the same; and for any speech or debate in either house, they shall not be questioned in any other place.

(2) No senator or representative shall, during the time for which he was elected, be appointed to any civil office under the authority of the United States, which shall have been created, or the emoluments whereof shall have been increased during such time; and no person holding any office under the United States shall be a member of either house during his continuance in office.

Section 7. (1) All bills for raising revenue shall originate in the House of Representatives; but the Senate may propose or concur with amendments as on other bills.

(2) Every bill which shall have passed the House of Representatives and the Senate, shall, before it become a law, be presented to the President of the United States; if he approve he shall sign it, but if not he shall return it, with his objections to that house in which it shall have originated, who shall enter the objections at large on their journal, and proceed to reconsider it. If after such reconsideration two-thirds of that house shall agree to pass the bill, it shall be sent, together with the objections, to the other house, by which it shall likewise be reconsidered, and if approved by two-thirds of that house, it shall become a law. But in all such cases the votes of both houses shall be determined by yeas and nays, and the names of the persons voting for and against the bill shall be entered on the journal of each house respectively. If any bill shall not be returned by the President within ten days (Sundays excepted) after it shall have been presented to him, the same shall be a law, in like manner as if he had signed it, unless the Congress by their

adjournment prevent its return, in which case it shall not be a law.

(3) Every order, resolution, or vote to which the concurrence of the Senate and House of Representatives may be necessary (except on a question of adjournment) shall be presented to the President of the United States; and before the same shall take effect, shall be approved by him, or being disapproved by him, shall be repassed by two-thirds of the Senate and House of Representatives, according to the rules and limitations prescribed in the case of a bill.

Powers Granted to Congress

The Congress shall have power:

Section 8. (1) To lay and collect taxes, duties, imposts and excises, to pay the debts and provide for the common defense and general welfare of the United States; but all duties, imposts and excises shall be uniform throughout the United States;

(2) To borrow money on the credit of the United States;

(3) To regulate commerce with foreign nations, and among the several states, and with the Indian tribes;

(4) To establish an uniform rule of naturalization, and uniform laws on the subject of bankruptcies throughout the United States;

(5) To coin money, regulate the value thereof, and of foreign coin, and fix the standard of weights and measures;

(6) To provide for the punishment of counterfeiting the securities and current coin of the United States;

(7) To establish post offices and post roads;

(8) To promote the progress of science and useful arts, by securing for limited times to authors and inventors the exclusive right to their respective writings and discoveries;

(9) To constitute tribunals inferior to the Supreme Court;

(10) To define and punish piracies and felonies committed on the high seas, and offenses against the law of nations;

(11) To declare war, grant letters of marque and reprisal, and make rules concerning captures on land and water;

(12) To raise and support armies, but no appropriation of money to that use shall be for a longer term than two years;

(13) To provide and maintain a navy;

(14) To make rules for the government and regulation of the land and naval forces;

(15) To provide for calling forth the militia to execute the laws of the Union, suppress insurrections and repel invasions;

(16) To provide for organizing, arming, and disciplining the militia, and for governing such part of them as may be employed in the service of the United States, reserving to the states respectively, the appointment of the officers, and the authority of training the militia according to the discipline prescribed by Congress;

(17) To exercise exclusive legislation in all cases whatsoever, over such district (not exceeding ten miles square) as may, by cession of particular states, and the acceptance of Congress, become the seat of the government of the United States, and to exercise like authority over all places purchased by the consent of the legislature of the state in which the same shall be, for the erection of forts, magazines, arsenals, dockyards, and other needful buildings;—And

(18) To make all laws which shall be necessary and proper for carrying into execution the foregoing powers, and all other powers vested by this Constitution in the government of the United States, or in any department or officer thereof.

Powers Forbidden to Congress

Section 9. (1) The migration or importation of such persons as any of the states now existing shall think proper to admit, shall not be prohibited by the Congress prior to the year one thousand eight hundred and eight, but a tax or duty may be imposed on such importation, not exceeding ten dollars for each person.

(2) The privilege of the writ of *habeas corpus* shall not be suspended, unless when in cases of rebellion or invasion the public safety may require it.

(3) No bill of attainder or *ex post facto* law shall be passed.

(4) No capitation, [or other direct,] tax shall be laid, unless in proportion to the census or enumeration herein before directed to be taken.

(5) No tax or duty shall be laid on articles exported from any state.

(6) No preference shall be given by any regulation of commerce or revenue to the ports of one state over those of another: nor shall vessels bound to, or from, one state, be obliged to enter, clear, or pay duties in another.

(7) No money shall be drawn from the treasury, but in consequence of appropriations made by law; and a regular statement and account of the receipts and expenditures of all public money shall be published from time to time.

(8) No title of nobility shall be granted by the United States: And no person holding any office or profit or trust under them, shall, without the consent of the Congress, accept of any present, emolument, office, or title, of any kind whatsoever, from any king, prince, or foreign state.

Powers Forbidden to the States

Section 10. (1) No state shall enter into any treaty, alliance, or confederation; grant letters of marque and reprisal; coin money; emit bills of credit; make any thing but gold and silver coin a tender in payment of debts; pass any bill of attainder, *ex post facto* law, or law impairing the obligation of contracts, or grant any title of nobility.

(2) No state shall, without the consent of the Congress, lay any imposts or duties on imports or exports, except what may be absolutely necessary for executing its inspection laws: and the net produce of all duties and imposts, laid by any state on imports or exports, shall be for the use of the treasury of the United States, and all such laws shall be subject to the revision and control of the Congress.

(3) No state shall, without the consent of Congress, lay any duty of tonnage, keep troops, or ships of war in time of peace, enter into any agreement or compact with another state, or with a foreign power, or engage in war, unless actually invaded, or in such imminent danger as will not admit of delay.

Article II
The Executive Branch

Section 1. (1) The executive power shall be vested in a President of the United States of America. He shall hold his office during the term of four years, and, together with the Vice President, chosen for the same term, be elected as follows:

(2) Each state shall appoint, in such manner as the legislature thereof may direct, a number of electors, equal to the whole number of senators and representatives to which the state may be entitled in the Congress: but no senator or representative, or person holding an office of trust or profit under the United States, shall be appointed an elector.

(3) [The electors shall meet in their respective states, and vote by ballot for two persons, of whom one at least shall not be an inhabitant of the same state with themselves. And they shall make a list of all the persons voted for, and of the number of votes for each; which list they shall sign and certify, and transmit sealed to the seat of government of the United States, directed to the president of the Senate. The president of the Senate shall, in the presence of the Senate and House of Representatives, open all the certificates, and the votes shall then be counted. The person having the greatest number of votes shall be the President, if such number be a majority of the whole number of electors appointed; and if there be more than one who have such majority, and have an equal number of votes, then the House of Representatives shall immediately choose by ballot one of them for President; and if no person have a majority, then from the five highest on the list the said House shall in like manner choose the President. But in choosing the President, the votes shall be taken by states, the representation from each state having one vote; a quorum for this purpose shall consist of a member or members from two-thirds of the states, and a majority of all the states shall be necessary to a choice. In every case, after the choice of the President, the person having the greatest number of votes of the electors shall be the Vice President. But if there should remain two or more who have equal votes, the Senate shall choose from them by ballot the Vice President.]

(4) The Congress may determine the time of choosing the electors, and the day on which they shall give their

votes; which day shall be the same throughout the United States.

(5) No person except a natural-born citizen, or a citizen of the United States, at the time of the adoption of this Constitution, shall be eligible to the office of President; neither shall any person be eligible to that office who shall not have attained to the age of thirty-five years, and been fourteen years a resident within the United States.

(6) In case of the removal of the President from office, or of his death, resignation, or inability to discharge the powers and duties of the said office, the same shall devolve on the Vice President, and the Congress may by law provide for the case of removal, death, resignation, or inability, both of the President and Vice President, declaring what officer shall then act as President, and such officer shall act accordingly, until the disability be removed, or a President shall be elected.

(7) The President shall, at stated times, receive for his services, a compensation, which shall neither be increased nor diminished during the period for which he shall have been elected, and he shall not receive within that period any other emolument from the United States, or any of them.

(8) Before he enter on the execution of his office, he shall take the following oath or affirmation: "I do solemnly swear (or affirm) that I will faithfully execute the office of the President of the United States, and will to the best of my ability, preserve, protect and defend the Constitution of the United States."

Section 2. (1) The President shall be commander-in-chief of the Army and Navy of the United States, and of the militia of the several states, when called into the actual service of the United States; he may require the opinion, in writing, of the principal officer in each of the executive departments, upon any subject relating to the duties of their respective offices, and he shall have power to grant reprieves and pardons for offenses against the United States, except in cases of impeachment.

(2) He shall have power, by and with the advice and consent of the Senate, to make treaties, provided two-thirds of the senators present concur; and he shall nominate, and by and with the advice and consent of the Senate, shall appoint ambassadors, other public ministers and consuls, judges of the Supreme Court, and all other officers of the United States, whose appointments are not herein otherwise provided for, and which shall be established by law: but the Congress may by law vest the appointment of such inferior officers, as they think proper, in the President alone, in the courts of law, or in the heads of departments.

(3) The President shall have the power to fill up all vacancies that may happen during the recess of the Senate, by granting commissions which shall expire at the end of their next session.

Section 3. He shall from time to time give to the Congress information of the state of the Union, and recommend to their consideration such measures as he shall judge necessary and expedient; he may, on extraordinary occasions, convene both houses, or either of them, and in case of disagreement between them, with respect to the time of adjournment, he may adjourn them to such time as he shall think proper; he shall receive ambassadors and other public ministers; he shall take care that the laws be faithfully executed, and shall commission all the officers of the United States.

Section 4. The President, Vice President and all civil officers of the United States, shall be removed from office on impeachment for, and conviction of, treason, bribery, or other high crimes and misdemeanors.

ARTICLE III
The Judicial Branch

Section 1. The judicial power of the United States, shall be vested in one Supreme Court, and in such inferior courts as the Congress may from time to time ordain and establish. The judges, both of the Supreme and inferior courts, shall hold their offices during good behaviour, and shall, at stated times, receive for their services, a compensation, which shall not be diminished during their continuance in office.

Section 2. (1) The judicial power shall extend to all cases, in law and equity, arising under this Constitution, the laws of the United States, and treaties made, or which shall be made, under their authority; —to all cases affecting ambassadors, other public ministers and consuls;—to all cases of admiralty and maritime jurisdiction;—to controversies to which the United States shall be a party;—to controversies between two or more states, [between a state and citizens of another state;], between citizens of different states;—between citizens of the same state claiming lands under grants of different states, and between a state, or the citizens thereof, and foreign states, [citizens or subjects].

(2) In all cases affecting ambassadors, other public ministers and consuls, and those in which a state shall be party, the Supreme Court shall have original jurisdiction. In all the other cases before mentioned, the Supreme Court shall have appellate jurisdiction, both as to law and fact, with such exceptions, and under such regulations as the Congress shall make.

(3) The trial of all crimes, except in cases of impeachment, shall be by jury; and such trial shall be held in the state where the said crimes shall have been committed; but when not committed within any state, the trial shall be at such place or places as the Congress may by law have directed.

Section 3. (1) Treason against the United States, shall consist only in levying war against them, or in adhering to their enemies, giving them aid and comfort. No person shall be convicted of treason unless on the testimony of two witnesses to the same overt act, or on confession in open court.

(2) The Congress shall have power to declare the punishment of treason, but no attainder of treason shall work corruption of blood, or forfeiture, except during the life of the person attainted.

ARTICLE IV
Relation of the States to Each Other

Section 1. Full faith and credit shall be given in each state to the public acts, records, and judicial proceedings of every other state. And the Congress may by general laws prescribe the manner in which such acts, records and proceedings shall be proved, and the effect thereof.

Section 2. (1) The citizens of each state shall be entitled to all privileges and immunities of citizens in the several states.

(2) A person charged in any state with treason, felony, or other crime, who shall flee justice, and be found in another state, shall on demand of the executive authority of the state from which he fled, be delivered up, to be removed to the state having jurisdiction of the crime.

(3) [No person held to service or labor in one state, under the laws thereof, escaping into another, shall, in consequence of any law or regulation therein, be discharged from such service or labor, but shall be delivered up on claim of the party to whom such service or labor may be due.]

Federal-State Relations

Section 3. (1) New states may be admitted by the Congress into this Union; but no new state shall be formed or erected within the jurisdiction of any other state, nor any state be formed by the junction of two or more states, without the consent of the legislatures of the states concerned as well as of the Congress.

(2) The Congress shall have power to dispose of and make all needful rules and regulations respecting the territory or other property belonging to the United States; and nothing in this Constitution shall be so construed as to prejudice any claims of the United States, or of any particular state.

Section 4. The United States shall guarantee to every state in this Union a republican form of government, and shall protect each of them against invasion; and on application of the legislature, or of the executive (when the legislature cannot be convened), against domestic violence.

ARTICLE V
Amending the Constitution

The Congress, whenever two-thirds of both houses shall deem it necessary, shall propose amendments to this Constitution, or, on the application of the legislatures of two-thirds of the several states, shall call a convention for proposing amendments, which, in either case, shall be valid to all intents and purposes, as part of this Constitution, when ratified by the legislatures of three-fourths of the several states, or by conventions in three-fourths thereof, as the one or the other mode of ratification may be proposed by the Congress; provided [that no amendment which may be made prior to the year one thousand eight hundred and eight, shall in any manner affect the first and fourth clauses in the ninth section of the first article; and] that no state, without its consent, shall be deprived of its equal suffrage in the Senate.

ARTICLE VI
National Debts

(1) All debts contracted and engagements entered into, before the adoption of this Constitution, shall be as

valid against the United States under this Constitution, as under the Confederation.

Supremacy of the National Government

(2) This Constitution, and the laws of the United States which shall be made in pursuance thereof; and all treaties made, or which shall be made, under the authority of the United States shall be the supreme law of the land; and the judges in every state shall be bound thereby, any thing in the constitution or laws of any state to the contrary notwithstanding.

(3) The senators and representatives before mentioned, and the members of the several state legislatures, and all executive and judicial officers, both of the United States and of the several states, shall be bound by oath or affirmation, to support this Constitution; but no religious test shall ever be required as a qualification to any office or public trust under the United States.

ARTICLE VII
Ratifying the Constitution

The ratification of the conventions of nine states, shall be sufficient for the establishment of this Constitution between the states so ratifying the same.

Done in convention by the unanimous consent of the states present the seventeenth day of September in the year of our Lord one thousand seven hundred and eighty-seven and of the independence of the United States of America the twelfth. In witness whereof we have hereunto subscribed our names.

Amendments to the Constitution

The first ten amendments, known as the Bill of Rights, were proposed on September 25, 1789. They were ratified, or accepted, on December 15, 1791. They were adopted because some states refused to approve the Constitution unless a Bill of Rights, protecting individuals from various unjust acts of government, was added.

Amendment 1

Freedom of religion, speech, and the press;
rights of assembly and petition

Amendment 2

Right to bear arms

Amendment 3

Housing of soldiers

Amendment 4

Search and arrest warrants

Amendment 5

Rights in criminal cases

Amendment 6

Rights to a fair trial

Amendment 7

Rights in civil cases

Amendment 8

Bails, fines, and punishments

Amendment 9

Rights retained by the people

Amendment 10

Powers retained by the states and the people

Amendment 11

Lawsuits against states

Amendment 12

Election of the President and Vice President

Amendment 13

Abolition of slavery

Amendment 14

Civil rights

Amendment 15
African-American suffrage

Amendment 16
Income taxes

Amendment 17
Direct election of senators

Amendment 18
Prohibition of liquor

Amendment 19
Women's suffrage

Amendment 20
Terms of the President and Congress

Amendment 21
Repeal of prohibition

Amendment 22
Presidential term limits

Amendment 23

Suffrage in the District of Columbia

Amendment 24

Poll taxes

Amendment 25

Presidential disability and succession

Amendment 26

Suffrage for eighteen-year-olds

Amendment 27

Congressional salaries

Chapter Notes

Chapter 1

1. Leon F. Litwack, *Been in the Storm So Long: The Aftermath of Slavery* (New York: Random House, Inc., 1979), p. 313.

2. Ibid.

3. Ibid., p. 311.

4. Peter J. Rachleff, *Black Labor in the South: Richmond, Virginia, 1865–1890* (Philadelphia: Temple University Press, 1984), pp. 19–20.

5. Ibid., p. 25.

6. W.E.B. Du Bois, *Black Reconstruction* (New York: Harcourt, Brace & Co., 1935), pp. 538–539.

7. Quoted in Rachleff, p. 25.

8. Quoted in Du Bois, p. 136.

9. Ibid., pp. 136–137.

10. Jerelyn Eddings and Eric Randall, "Free at Last," *U.S. News & World Report*, May 9, 1994, p. 30.

11. Rachleff, p. 37.

12. Ibid., p. 38.

13. Litwack, p. 531.

14. Rachleff, p. 41.

15. Ibid.

16. Litwack, p. 548.

17. Page Smith, *Trial by Fire: A People's History of the Civil War and Reconstruction* (New York: Viking Penguin Books, 1982), p. 739.

Chapter 2

1. Farah Mounir and Andrea Berens Karls, *World History: The Human Experience* (Columbus, Ohio: Glencoe Company, 1994), p. 274.

2. Marchette Chute, *The First Liberty: A History of the Right to Vote in America, 1619–1850* (New York: Dutton, 1969), p. 141.

3. Quoted in Chilton Williamson, *American Suffrage: From Property to Democracy 1760–1860* (Princeton, N.J.: Princeton University Press, 1960), pp. 5–6.

4. Chute, p. 141.

5. Williamson, pp. 25–39.
6. Ibid., p. 219.
7. Quoted in Chute, p. 293.
8. Williamson, p. 242.
9. Paul Lewinson, *Race, Class & Party: A History of Negro Suffrage and White Politics in the South* (New York: Russell & Russell, 1963), p. 82.
10. Jerelyn Eddings and Eric Randall, "Free at Last," *U.S. News & World Report*, May 9, 1994, p. 30.

Chapter 3

1. Lerone Bennett, Jr., *Before the Mayflower: A History of Black America* (Chicago: Johnson Publishing Co., 1987), p. 29.
2. Ibid., p 41.
3. Benjamin Quarles, *The Negro in the Making of America*, rev. ed. (New York: Collier Books, 1969), p. 34.
4. Bennett, p. 45.
5. Quoted in E. Franklin Frazier, *The Negro in the United States* (New York: Macmillan Publishing Co. Inc., 1957), pp. 23–24.
6. Ibid., p. 23.
7. Ibid., p. 26.
8. Bennett, p. 46.
9. John Blassingame, *The Slave Community: Plantation Life in the Antebellum South*, rev. and enlarged ed. (New York: Oxford University Press, 1979), p. 17.
10. Irwin Unger, *The Slavery Experience in the United States* (New York: Holt, Rinehart & Winston Publishing Co., 1970), pp. 19–20.
11. Ibid., p. 20.
12. Quarles, p. 48.
13. Bennett, p. 38.
14. Ibid., p. 69.
15. Quoted in Melvin Drimmer, ed., *Black History: A Reappraisal* (New York: Doubleday & Company, Inc., 1968), p. 99.
16. Ibid., p. 129.
17. Avery Craven, *Reconstruction: The Ending of the Civil War* (New York: Holt, Rinehart and Winston Publishing Co., 1969), p. 262.
18. Ira Berlin, *Slaves Without Masters: The Free Negro in the Antebellum South* (New York: Pantheon Books, 1974), p. 397.

19. Quoted in Blassingame, p. 257.

20. Ibid., p. 263.

21. Quoted in Eric L. McKitrick, ed., *Slavery Defended: The Views of the Old South* (Englewood Cliffs, N.J.: Prentice Hall Publishers, 1963), p. 18.

22. Ibid, pp. 37–38.

23. Alexis de Tocqueville, *Democracy in America,* trans. Henry Reeve (New York: Dutton, 1976), vol. 1, p. 359.

24. David Herbert Donald, *Lincoln* (New York: Simon & Schuster, 1995), p. 221.

25. James H. Dormon and Robert R. Jones, *The Afro-American Experience: A Cultural History Through Emancipation* (New York: John Wiley and Sons, 1974), p. 232.

26. Robert Cruden, *The Negro in Reconstruction* (Englewood Cliffs, N.J.: Prentice Hall Publishers, 1969), p. 6.

27. Eric Foner, *Reconstruction: America's Unfinished Revolution, 1863–1877* (New York: Harper & Row, 1988), p. 294.

28. Quoted in Cruden, p. 59.

29. Page Smith, *Trial By Fire: A People's History of the Civil War and Reconstruction* (New York: McGraw-Hill, 1982), p. 739.

30. Quoted in John Hope Franklin, *Reconstruction: After the Civil War* (Chicago: University of Chicago Press, 1961), p. 124.

31. Quoted in Foner, p. 287.

32. Franklin, pp. 88–89.

33. Quoted in Frazier, p. 134.

34. Ibid., p. 128.

35. Brenda Stalcup, ed., *Reconstruction: Opposing Viewpoints* (San Diego: Greenhaven Press, 1995), p. 148.

36. Cruden, p. 19.

37. Smith, pp. 707–708.

38. Franklin, pp. 63–64.

39. Ibid., pp. 62–64.

40. W.E.B. Du Bois, *Black Reconstruction in America* (New York: Harcourt, Brace & Co., 1935), p. 226.

41. Ibid., p. 219.

42. Hans L. Trefousse, *Reconstruction: America's First Effort at Racial Democracy* (New York: Van Nostrand Reinhold, 1971), pp. 103–114.

43. Ibid.

44. Smith, p. 738.
45. Leon F. Litwack, *Been in the Storm So Long: The Aftermath of Slavery* (New York: Random House, Inc., 1979), p. 546.
46. Foner, p. 289.
47. Ibid., p. 291.
48. Ibid., p. 318.
49. Franklin, p. 102.
50. Quoted in Du Bois, p. 389.
51. Ibid., pp. 389–390.
52. Quoted in Foner, p. 303.
53. Ibid., p. 426.
54. Smith, p. 740.
55. Quoted in Du Bois, p. 627

Chapter 4

1. Steven F. Lawson, *Black Ballots: Voting Rights in the South, 1944–1969* (New York: Columbia University Press, 1976), p. 1
2. W.E.B. Du Bois, *Black Reconstruction* (Millwood, N.Y.: Kraus-Thomson Organization, Ltd., 1976), p. 257.
3. William Gillette, *The Right to Vote: Politics and the Passage of the Fifteenth Amendment* (Baltimore: Johns Hopkins University Press, 1969), pp. 25–26.
4. Quoted in Avery Craven, *Reconstruction: The Ending of the Civil War* (New York: Holt, Rinehart & Winston, 1969), p. 263.
5. Quoted in C. Vann Woodward, "The Political Legacy of Reconstruction," in *Black History: A Reappraisal*, ed. Melvin Drimmer (New York: Doubleday, 1968), p. 296.
6. Ibid., p. 276.
7. Quoted in Du Bois, p. 209.
8. Quoted in Page Smith, *Trial by Fire: A People's History of the Civil War and Reconstruction* (New York: McGraw-Hill Book Company, 1982), p. 736.
9. Brenda Stalcup, ed., *Reconstruction: Opposing Viewpoints* (San Diego: Greenwood Press, 1995), p. 49.
10. Craven, p. 25.
11. Eric Foner, *The Life and Writings of Frederick Douglass* (New York: International Publishers, 1955), vol. 4, p. 161.
12. Smith, p. 347.
13. Du Bois, p. 538.

14. Henrietta Buckmaster, *Freedom Bound* (New York: Macmillan Publishing Co., 1965), p. 43.

15. Smith, p. 817.

16. Du Bois, p. 309.

17. Gillette, p. 46.

18. Ibid., pp. 46, 50.

19. Smith, p. 818.

20. Quoted in Gillette, p. 59.

21. James Z. George, *The Political History of Slavery in the United States* (New York: Negro University Press, 1969), p. 242.

22. LaWanda Cox and John H. Cox, eds., *Reconstruction, the Negro and the New South* (Columbia, S.C.: University of South Carolina Press, 1973), p. 106.

23. Ibid., pp. 65–66.

24. United States Constitution, Amendment Fifteen, ratified February 3, 1870.

25. Cox and Cox, p. 79.

26. Ibid., pp. 81–89

27. Quoted in Gillette, p. 161.

28. Quoted in Du Bois, p. 594.

29. Ibid.

Chapter 5

1. Eric Foner, *Reconstruction: America's Unfinished Revolution, 1863–1877* (New York: Harper & Row, 1988), p. 449.

2. David Chalmers, *Hooded Americanism: A History of the Ku Klux Klan* (Durham, N.C.: Duke University Press, 1987), pp. 8–9.

3. John Hope Franklin, *Reconstruction: After the Civil War* (Chicago: University of Chicago Press, 1961), p. 154.

4. Herbert Aptheker, ed., *A Documentary History of the Negro People in the United States* (New York: Citadel Press, 1969), pp. 595–596.

5. Franklin, pp. 159–160.

6. Smith, p. 846.

7. Quoted in Foner, p. 428.

8. Chalmers, p. 14.

9. Page Smith, *Trial by Fire: A People's History of the Civil War and Reconstruction* (New York: McGraw-Hill, 1982), p. 855.

10. Franklin, p. 168.

11. Chalmers, p. 15.

12. Henrietta Buckmaster, *Freedom Bound* (New York: Macmillan Publishing Co., 1965), p. 122.

13. Foner, pp. 558–562.

14. Smith, p. 914.

15. Steven F. Lawson, *Black Ballots: Voting Rights in the South, 1944–1969* (New York: Columbia University Press, 1976), pp. 4, 6.

16. Paul Lewinson, *Race, Class, & Party: A History of Negro Suffrage and White Politics in the South* (New York: Russell & Russell Publishing Co., 1963), p. 64.

17. W.E.B. Du Bois, *Black Reconstruction* (Millwood, N.Y.: Kraus-Thomson Organization, Ltd., 1976), p. 589.

18. Quoted in John R. Lynch, *The Facts of Reconstruction* (New York: Arno Press & The New York Times, 1968), p. 263.

19. Lewinson, p. 86.

20. Loren Miller, *The Petitioners: The Story of the Supreme Court of the United States and the Negro* (New York: Pantheon Press, 1966), p. 218.

Chapter 6

1. Loren Miller, *The Petitioners: The Story of the Supreme Court of the United States and the Negro* (New York: Pantheon Press, 1966), p. 218.

2. Paul Lewison, *Race, Class, and Party: A History of Negro Suffrage and White Politics in the South* (New York: Russell & Russell Publishing Inc., 1963), p. 114.

3. Ibid., p. 107.

4. Philip S. Foner, ed., *W.E.B. Du Bois Speaks: Speeches and Addresses, 1920–1963* (New York: Pathfinder Press, 1970), pp. 36–37.

5. Miller, p. 298.

6. Lewinson, p. 118.

7. Ibid., p. 162.

8. Miller, p. 298.

9. William Gillette, *The Right to Vote: Politics and the Passage of the Fifteenth Amendment* (Baltimore: Johns Hopkins University Press, 1969), p. 10.

10. Quoted in Steven F. Lawson, *Black Ballots: Voting Rights in the South, 1944–1969* (New York: Columbia University Press, 1976), pp. 119–120.

11. Lewinson, p. 119.

12. Lawson, p. 341.

13. Charles Evers, *Evers* (New York: World Press, 1971), pp. 93–94.

14. Miller, p. 301.

15. Henry Hampton and Steve Fayer, with Sarah Flynn, *Voices of Freedom: An Oral History of the Civil Rights Movement from the 1950s Through the 1980s* (New York: Bantam Books Inc., 1990), p. 2.

16. Ibid.

17. Quoted in Ibid., pp. 177–178.

18. Quoted in Merle Miller, *Lyndon: An Oral Biography* (New York: G.P. Putnam's Sons, 1980), p. 367.

19. Lawson, p. 267.

20. Ibid., p. 217.

21. Miller, p. 367.

22. Quoted in Lawson, p. 321.

23. Ibid., pp. 329–330.

24. Ibid.

25. Ibid., p. 337.

26. Ibid., p. 330.

27. Ibid., pp. 130–131.

28. David A. Bositis, "Blacks and the 1996 Elections: A Preliminary Analysis" (Washington, D.C.: National Coalition of Black Voter Participation, 1996), p. 1.

29. *World Almanac* (Mahwah, N.J.: World Almanac Books, 1997), p. 379.

30. Chandler Davidson and Bernard Grofman, eds., *Quiet Revolution in the South: The Impact of the Voting Rights Act, 1965–1990* (Princeton, N.J.: Princeton University Press, 1994), p. 386.

31. Author conversation with Dennis Rogers of the National Coalition of Black Voter Participation, December, 1996.

Glossary

abolitionist—A person who was in favor of doing away with slavery in the United States.

amendment—A revision or addition to a law or to the United States Constitution.

civil rights—The rights guaranteed to all Americans by the Thirteenth, Fourteenth, and Fifteenth Amendments to the Constitution. These rights include equal treatment under the law, the right not to be enslaved, and the right to vote.

convention—An assembly called for a specific purpose, such as selecting a candidate for a political office, drafting a constitution, or formulating new policies.

discrimination—Showing prejudice toward a certain group of people, by treating those people differently.

disenfranchise—To deprive someone of the right to vote.

freeholder—A land owner.

Jim Crow laws—Laws that mandated the use of separate facilities for blacks and whites in such public places as restaurants, hotels, barbershops, and railroad cars.

poll tax—A fee a person must pay in order to vote.

primary—An election in which members of a political party select their candidates for office.

property requirement—The stipulation that a person must own property, usually of at least a certain minimum value, in order to be allowed to vote.

ratification—Giving official approval, passing.

Reconstruction—The period of growth following the Civil War during which the southern states were reorganized and readmitted to the Union.

registrar—An official who signs people up so that they can vote.

suffrage—The right to vote.

Further Reading

Archer, Jules. *They Had a Dream: The Civil Rights Struggle, From Frederick Douglass to Marcus Garvey to Martin Luther King, and Malcolm X.* New York: Viking Press, 1993.

Buckmaster, Henrietta. *Freedom Bound.* New York: Macmillan, 1965.

Fireside, Harvey, and Sarah Betsy Fuller. *Brown v. Board of Education: Equal Schooling for All.* Springfield, N.J.: Enslow Publishers, Inc., 1994.

Foner, Eric. *Reconstruction: America's Unfinished Revolution, 1863–1877.* New York: Harper & Row, 1988.

Franklin, John Hope. *From Slavery to Freedom: A History of African Americans.* New York: McGraw-Hill Publishing Co., 1994.

Haskins, James S. *The March on Washington.* New York: HarperCollins Publishers, 1993.

Herda, D. J. *The Dred Scott Case: Slavery and Citizenship.* Springfield, N.J.: Enslow Publishers, Inc., 1994.

Lucas, Eileen. *Civil Rights: The Long Struggle.* Springfield, N.J.: Enslow Publishers, Inc., 1996.

Miller, Marilyn. *The Bridge at Selma.* Morristown, N.J.: Silver Burdett Press, 1985.

Myers, Walter Dean. *Now Is Your Time!* The African-American Struggle for Freedom. New York: Scholastic, 1992.

Newman, Gerald, and Eleanor Newman Layfield. *Racism: Divided by Color.* Springfield, N.J.: Enslow Publishers, Inc., 1995.

Powledge, Fred. *We Shall Overcome: Heroes of the Civil Rights Movement.* New York: Simon & Schuster Children's Publishers, 1993.

Russell, Charman. *Frederick Douglass.* New York: Chelsea House Publishers, 1988.

Smith, Carter, ed. *One Nation Again: A Sourcebook on the Civil War.* Brookfield, Conn.: Millbrook Press, 1993.

Index